BLESSED ARE THE PURE IN HEART

by
DANIEL BOURGUET

Translated from the French

THE PEOPLE'S SEMINARY PRESS

BLESSED ARE THE PURE IN HEART

The People's Seminary Press
Burlington, WA 98233
www.peoplesseminary.org
ISBN: 978-1-954387-14-0

Translated from the original French edition.
Daniel Bouguet, Lyon: Éditions Olivétan, 2005.
Copyright @ 2005 Éditions Olivétan, Lyon, France.

Bible passages are literal translations of the French. The author uses a range of French translations.

A full list of books by Daniel Bourguet together with details of those works which have been published in English is available at www.danielbourguet.com

CONTENTS

Translator's Note   vii

Foreword by Bob Ekblad   ix

Preface   xvii

    Chapter 1– Impurity of heart   1

    Chapter 2– Asking for cleansing   43

    Chapter 3– Tears of cleansing   75

Translator's Note

IN SOME INSTANCES THERE ARE IDIOMS IN FRENCH THAT are difficult to translate, but that has not generally been the case with this book. Further to the author's original notes some translator's notes have been added as footnotes; they are generally glosses of the French but sometimes are of a more explanatory nature; the notes have been endorsed by the author. Biblical passages are mostly the translator's version of the French since the point might otherwise be lost.

In keeping with the other translations in this series, a substantial effort has been made to employ "gender neutral" terms. The modern sensitivity in this area is not something that is found in the French or the translator's background, so it hasn't always been easy.

Please see www.danielbourguet.com
for further details

FOREWORD

THE PUBLICATION OF DANIEL BOURGUET'S BOOKS IN English is a valuable contribution to the literature of contemplative theology and spirituality that will nourish and inspire the faith of all who read them. Daniel Bourguet, a French Protestant pastor and theologian of the Huguenot tradition, lives as a monk in the mountainous Cévennes region in the south of France. There at his hermitage near Saint-Jean-du-Gard, Daniel maintains a daily rhythm of prayer, worship, Scripture reading, theological reflection, and spiritual accompaniment. All of his books flow out of a life steeped in love of God, Scripture, and the seekers who come to him for spiritual support.

I first met Daniel Bourguet in 1988 when my wife, Gracie, and I moved from rural Central America to study theology at the Institut Protestant de Théologie (IPT), where he taught Old Testament. The IPT is the Église Réformée de France's[1] denominational graduate school in Montpellier, France.

Prior to our move to France, while ministering among impoverished farmers in Honduras in the 1980s, we came across the writings of the Swiss theologian Wilhelm

1. Now Église Protestante Unie de France.

Vischer and the French theologian Daniel Lys by way of footnotes in Jacques Ellul's inspiring books. Vischer had written a three-volume work entitled *The Witness of the Old Testament to Christ*, of which only volume 1 is translated into English.[2] That book, along with a number of articles and Daniel Lys' brilliant *The Meaning of the Old Testament*,[3] exposed us to a community of Bible scholars who articulated a continuity between the Old and New Testaments that was highly relevant both then and now. This connection ultimately led me to Bourguet.

We experienced firsthand how a literal reading of the Old Testament in isolation from the New Testament confession that Jesus is both Lord and Christ (Messiah) brings great confusion, division, and even destruction. In rural Honduras churches often distinguish themselves by selectively observing Old Testament laws and using certain Old Testament stories to inspire fear of God as a punishing judge. North American Christians at this time were drawing from the Old Testament to justify the death penalty and US military intervention in Central America and beyond.

Wilhelm Vischer, an active resister of Nazism from his Old Testament teaching post inside Germany, resisted the misuse of Scripture to justify anti-Semitism, nationalism, and war, insisting on the importance of the Old Testament for Christian faith at a time when it was being dismissed. He was consequently one of the first professors of theology to be pressured to leave his post and eventually depart Nazi Germany before World War II. He served as Karl

2. Wilhelm Vischer, *The Witness of the Old Testament to Christ*, vol. 1, *The Pentateuch*, trans. A. B. Crabtree (London: Lutterworth, 1949).

3. Daniel Lys, *The Meaning of the Old Testament* (Nashville: Abingdon, 1967).

Barth's pastor in Basel after he, too, left Germany. After the war, the church in France, having been widely engaged in resistance to Nazism and deeply encouraged by Barth, invited Vischer to be the professor of Old Testament at the IPT in Montpellier.

The biblical reflections of Ellul, Vischer, Lys and other French theologians led Gracie and I to look into theological study in France.[4] We wrote the IPT about their graduate program and discovered that Vischer had long since retired after training several generations of pastors. His protégée, Daniel Lys, had recently retired but was still available. Lys's place had been filled by his doctoral student, Daniel Bourguet, who also had been trained by Vischer. The IPT welcomed us with a generous scholarship, and we soon made plans to learn French and move to Montpellier.

After being immersed in Bible studies with impoverished farmers in war-torn Honduras, we were eager for help in understanding Scripture. Disillusioned with America after being engaged in resisting US policy in Central America, we felt drawn to reflect from a different context. We reasoned that studying in a Protestant seminary with a history of persecution in a majority Catholic context would prove valuable. We left Tierra Nueva in the hands of local Honduran leaders and moved to Montpellier in July 1988 to study French and then began classes in September

Daniel Bourguet taught us Hebrew and Old Testament in ways that made the language and text come alive. He invited students into his passion and curiosity as we

4. We assumed there were others where these came from, and were able to study with pastor and New Testament professor Michel Bouttier, who was also trained by Vischer and published broadly, including a commentary on Ephesians and a number of collections of provocative articles. Elian Cuvillier followed Bouttier as Professor of New Testament at the IPT, writing many high quality books and articles.

pondered both familiar and difficult passages of Scripture. I remember continually being surprised at how seriously Daniel took every textual critical variant, even seemingly irrelevant ones. He masterfully invited and guided us to both scrutinize and contemplate each variant in its original language until we understood the angle from which ancient interpreters had viewed the text. Daniel modeled an honoring of distinct perspectives as we studied the history of interpretation of each passage. He sought to hold diverse perspectives together whenever possible, yet only embraced what the text actually permitted, exemplifying fine-tuned discernment that inspired us.

Daniel's thorough approach meant he would only take us through a chapter or two per semester. This mean we took entire courses on Genesis 1–2:4, on Abraham's call in Genesis 12:1-4, and on Jeremiah 31, Exodus 1–2, Psalms 1–2 and others. In each of his courses he included relevant rabbinic exegesis, New Testament use of the Old Testament, and the church fathers' interpretations. Daniel imparted his confidence that God speaks good news now as he accompanied us in our reading, making our hearts burn like those of the disciples of Emmaus, and inspiring us to want to do this with others. In alignment with Vischer and Lys he demonstrated through detailed exegesis of Old Testament texts how God's most total revelation in Jesus both fulfills and explains these Scriptures, making them come alive through the Holy Spirit in our lives and diverse contexts.

While living in France, Gracie and I traveled to Honduras every summer, spending several weeks sharing our learning with Tierra Nueva's Honduran leadership and leading Bible studies in rural villages before returning for classes in the fall. We pursued our studies in France with the vision of bringing the best scholarship to the service of the least in a deliberate effort to bridge the divide between the academy and the poor. Our experience of Daniel's rare blend of scholarship and pastoral sensitivity, which you will see for yourself in his books, contributed to us feeling called back to the church, into ordained ministry, and back to the US to teach and minister there. I benefited from having Daniel as my dissertation supervisor and continued to integrate regular study into our ministry of accompanying immigrants and inmates when we launched Tierra Nueva in Washington State.

Daniel Bourguet's writings are like high-quality wine extracted from vineyards planted in challenged soil. Born in 1946 in Aumessas, a small village in the Cévennes region of France, Daniel grew up in the heartland of Huguenot Protestantism, which issued from the Reformation in the sixteenth century. He pursued studies of theology at the IPT in Montpellier, including study in Germany, Switzerland and at the Ecole Biblique in Jerusalem. In lieu of military service, Daniel served as a teacher in Madagascar for a year. He was ordained as a pastor in the Église Réformée de France in 1972, serving parishes from 1973 to 1987. Daniel wrote his doctoral dissertation[5] while serving as a full-time parish pastor—a common practice in minority Protestant France, where teaching positions are scarce and pastors are in high demand. This practice often proves fruitful for ordinary Christians and theologians alike, deepening reflection and anchoring theologians in the church and world.

During our residential studies in Montpellier from 1988 to 1991, Gracie and I witnessed Daniel's interest in the early monastics and fathers of the Eastern Church grow. In 1991 Daniel became prior of La Fraternité Spirituelle des

5. See Daniel Bourguet, Des métaphores de Jérémie, Paris : J. Gabalda, 1987

Veilleurs (Spiritual Fraternity of the Watchpersons) and felt called to be a full-time monk, leaving the IPT in 1995 for a year in a Cistercian monastery in Lyon before moving to his current site in Les Cévennes in 1996.

Joy, simplicity, and mercy are the three pillars of Les Veilleurs, an association of laypeople and pastors founded by French Reformed pastor Wilfred Monod in 1923 (with a Francophone membership of four hundred in 2013). Members of this fellowship commit to pursuing daily rhythms of prayer and Scripture reading, including noontime recitation of the Beatitudes, Friday meditation on the cross, regular engagement with a faith community on Sundays, and spiritual retreats and reading that benefits from universal devotional and monastic practices. Les Veilleurs has served to nourish renewal in France and influenced the founding of communities such as Taizé. Under Daniel Bourguet's leadership Les Veilleurs thrived. As a member of Les Veilleurs myself I attended many of his annual retreats, witnessing and experiencing the vitality of this movement firsthand.

Since Daniel's departure from his professorship at the IPT in 1995, his teaching and writing have focused primarily on equipping ordinary Christians to grow spiritually through engaging in devotional practices such as prayer, Scripture reading and contemplation. Other works that will hopefully appear in English include reflections on asceticism, silence, daily prayer and the Trinity. All but three of Daniel's twenty-five or so books are based on spiritual retreats he offered to pastors and retreatants with Les Veilleurs. He has offered retreats to Roman Catholic, Orthodox, and Protestant communities throughout France and Francophone Europe and is widely read and appreciated as a theologian who bridges divergent worlds and nourishes faithful Christian practice in France. Daniel Bourguet made his first and only visit to the United States in 2005, offering a spiritual retreat in Washington State. He accompanied me to Honduras on that same trip just after Hurricane Katrina ravaged the country, teaching Tierra Nueva's leaders and accompanying me as I led Bible studies and ministered in rural communities.

Daniel left his role as prior in 2012 and now continues his daily offices, receives many seekers for personal retreats, and offers occasional retreats where he lives and writes. In alignment with the early monastic commitment to manual labor, Daniel weaves black and white wool tapestries of illustrations of biblical stories done by pastor and painter Henri Lindegaard. Daniel's unique contribution includes his Trinitarian approach to biblical interpretation, wherein he reads Scripture informed by the early church fathers with special sensitivity to how texts bear witness directly and indirectly to Jesus, the Father and the Holy Spirit.

Daniel Bourguet models an approach to Scripture and spirituality that is desperately needed in our times. He reads the Bible with great confidence in God's goodness, discovering through careful reading, prayer, and contemplation insights that feed faith and inspire practice. Daniel's deliberate reading in communion with the church fathers brings the wisdom of the ages to nourish the body of Christ today. His tender love for people who come to him for spiritual support as well as the larger church and world informs every page of his writing. May you find in this book refreshment, strength, and inspiration for your journey as you are drawn into deeper encounters with God.

Bob Ekblad
Mount Vernon, WA

PREFACE

THIS BOOK REPRISES STUDIES GIVEN DURING THE COURSE of 2003 at retreats for *La Fraternité spirituelle des Veilleurs*; they were also presented on other similar occasions, such as the retreat at Crêt-Bérard in Switzerland. At retreats, as with preaching, bibliographic references are not so important; they might have had a place in marginal notes, but I have preferred to keep them to a minimum with the idea of staying close to the style of a retreat, as if the reader was invited through this book into the retreat.

The people present at these retreats were believers, Christians, and the reader will see that my remarks assume this. Nothing has been changed, so a reader who is not a believer will undoubtedly feel uncertain at times; I can only apologize for all the questions that might arise and are left unanswered, but to go on a retreat is to retire from the world for a time to be face to face with God, and the teaching at a retreat is a means to that encounter; for this, a person would have to be a believer. This needs to be understood before reading the book; I am speaking here as if at a retreat, to a reader who is a believer.

Finally, again as if on a retreat, I have kept the elements of an oral style. You are addressed here as a "reader friend," as though in a dialogue, a dialogue which proposes to be no more than an overture to the most sublime of dialogues, dialogue with God.

So there we are, my reader friend! May your relationship with God find something here to nourish it.

Chapter 1

IMPURITY OF HEART

As he was journeying towards Jerusalem, Jesus passed through Samaria and Galilee. As he entered a village, ten lepers came out to meet him. They stood at a distance and, lifting up their voices, said, "Jesus, Master, have mercy on us!" Looking at them, Jesus said, "Go and show yourselves to the priests." As they were going, they were cleansed. One of them, seeing that he was healed, turned back, glorifying God in a loud voice; he fell on his face at Jesus' feet, giving him thanks. He was a Samaritan. Jesus, in response, said, "Were there not ten who were cleansed? Where are the other nine? Is only this stranger to be found giving glory to God?" Then he said to him, "Arise and go your way. Your faith has saved you." (Luke 17:11-19)

THIS PASSAGE IS UNIQUE, HAVING NO PARALLEL IN THE other Gospels. We therefore need to approach it very carefully because we can't lean on any account other than this of Luke. May the Lord lead us as we read!

The scene takes place between Samaria and Galilee, which is to say, a less-frequented, frontier zone, where the inhabitants of the two areas did not associate much. This somewhat wilderness area was therefore indicated as a home for undesirables who had to live apart from others,

1

lepers for example, whom the Law obligated to cut themselves off from the rest of the community. It is quite probable that the ten lepers originated from the two neighboring regions and were therefore Samaritans and Galileans.

The law concerning leprosy is found in the Pentateuch, in Leviticus 13. It was exactly the same for all ten lepers since the Pentateuch had the same divine authority for the Samaritans as it did for Galileans. To the Samaritan leper who came back to Jesus any reference to the Law meant just the same as it did to the nine others.

The passage in the law about leprosy is very lengthy, indicating the importance then accorded to this malady. I will cite from the passage two verses which give a good sense of the whole. "The leper is to wear his garments torn and have his head uncovered. He must cover the lower part of his face[1] and cry out, "Unclean, unclean!"[2] As long as he has the disease he shall be unclean. He is impure. He is to live alone; his place must be outside the camp" (Lev 13:45-46).

In just two verses the word "unclean" appears four times; this is a lot and very significant. It is a fact; a leprous person is unclean, indeed particularly unclean, and leprosy in Israel was one of the greatest impurities.

Impurity and banishment

Before going any further it is essential to define what characterizes impurity in the Bible. It appears clearly in this passage: it is whatever cuts off from God and from others. Whatever their impurity might be, every person who is unclean or impure is obligated by the Law to be separated

1. The French, with some English translations, reads "the upper lip." (Trans.)

2. Unclean – the French is *impur*. Throughout this passage the ideas of clean and pure, unclean and impure are interchangeable. (Trans.)

from others in order not to contaminate them. Whoever touches something unclean becomes unclean. Anyone who so much as touches an object that has been in contact with an unclean person becomes unclean.

This conception of impurity, which is foundational to the Law of Israel, is very severe; it means that an unclean person is truly an exile, cast out! To make this clear to us, reader friend, impurity is not considered in the Bible simply as a moral issue but impacts the relational level. This is how it will be viewed throughout this study. Impurity affects and disturbs all human relations and even relations with God; it weakens them to the point of their destruction. The unclean person, whatever the source of the impurity, can no longer live with others, not even with God.

All that we have just said springs readily from the text in the Law: it is specified that a leper had to stay "outside the camp", meaning apart from the human community. If he (or she) should meet with a healthy person, he had immediately to "cry out," from as far off as he could, as a warning to keep a good distance, "unclean, unclean."

Before crying out, he even had to "cover his lower face," that is, to cover his mouth with his hand so that no spittle or breath could reach and contaminate the healthy person.

Cut off from others, the person was also cut off from God. The statement that a person had to go "bare-headed" means that they were forbidden to pray because, in Israel, prayer required that the head be covered. What remained of any relationship with God if prayer was no longer possible?

Cut off from others and from God, the leper was in an extreme position, somewhere in between the living and the dead. This explains why he was required to have his clothing "rent"; this detail makes clear that his was an attitude of mourning. Every person in mourning, in fact, wore clothing that they had themselves torn at the moment of a loved one's death. The leper was therefore in a condition of mourning over every human relationship as well as their relationship with God. On the borderlands of Samaria, the ten lepers were exiles, neither living nor dead.

The succor of prayer

From the outset of the account, the ten lepers are presented as very respectful towards the Law. The Evangelist tells us that "they stood at a distance." Further, when they spoke they "lifted up their voices," which is right in line with the Law, but nonetheless with a slight but very interesting deviation, leading to the discovery that, while obeying the Law, they were also side-stepping it. Instead of crying out, "unclean, unclean!" to keep Jesus at a distance, they cried "Have mercy on us!" which clearly is not a way of repelling but of attracting the mercy of Jesus. So, even as they put Jesus on his guard by speaking to him from a distance, they were also pleading with him to draw near, if only in terms of extending his mercy and compassion. The suffering of these lepers was such that they dared to transgress the Law. Their cry was not so much a warning as a prayer, even though, bare-headed as they were, they had no right to pray! The impossible prayer suddenly becomes possible in the presence of Jesus! How wonderful! It is even more wonderful that Jesus both welcomes and fulfils this outside-the-Law prayer!

This surprising declension from cry into prayer is subtly suggested by Luke as he puts aside the verb "cry" used in the Law and replaces it with the expression "lift the voice," which, from this evangelist's pen, is a phrase belonging to the vocabulary of prayer. In Luke's writings, when someone "raises the voice," the purpose is prayer (cf. Acts 4:24). It is therefore clear; these bare-headed men, forbidden to pray, were applying themselves to prayer! In these men's hearts an inversion was taking place; they were not pushing Jesus away but, on the contrary, seeking to enter relationship with him, calling for his attention: "Jesus, master, have mercy on us!"

Unable to pray to God, it was to Jesus that the lepers turned, addressing their supplication to him. Their prayer allows a glimpse of the astonishing faith within them. In this faith, the great distress of men cast out by everyone finds expression: "Jesus, master, have mercy on us!" Who, then, was Jesus in their eyes that they would dare brave the holy Law and speak such a prayer?

Metal or glass

For lepers, the day they were cleansed was the end of an exile, the end of a nightmare. It was leaving hell behind, a return to the land of the living, to God and to human company. Their thirst for cleansing was particularly intense, and contrasts with another thirst we find in the Gospels, the desires of the Pharisees. We should highlight this difference so that we can understand Jesus' reaction to the two types of thirst.

The Pharisees were markedly attentive to anything that touched on purity, and scrupulously observant of every law related to this issue. They were the law's champions, but they sought purity to make a show of it and to look good in the eyes of others. For them, purity was an end in itself. We could compare this purity to the purity of metal. The purer a metal is, the shinier it becomes and the more it attracts attention from others. Jesus was to prove very severe with this hypocritical purity of the Pharisees: "Woe unto you who are like whited sepulchers, which look beautiful outwardly, but inwardly are full of dead men's bones and every type of impurity" (Matt 23:27).

With the lepers, things were quite different. Purity or cleansing was not for them an end in itself but a stage, a necessary passage to negotiate before rejoining the world of the healthy and God. A leper aspiring to cleansing did so of necessity, in order to recover his identity as a person, to enjoy loving relations with others and with God. In this case, the desired purity is comparable not to that of metal but of glass. The purer the glass, the more transparent it is and the less it attracts attention. The purer it is, the more it allows sight beyond it, through it. Where pure metal corresponds to vanity, pure glass is an example of humility. With the lepers' thirst for cleansing, Jesus reacts quite differently than he does to the Pharisees and their desire for purity.

"Go and show yourselves to the priests"

In Jesus' response to the plea of the ten lepers we may at first hear a somewhat incomplete reception of it. If we compare it with his response to another leper, the difference is striking. With this other leper, Jesus made free to touch him, said, "I will; be clean!" and then sent him to the priest to follow the ritual prescriptions of the Law (Luke 5:13-14). Here things are quite different; Jesus simply sent the lepers to the priests. He neither touched them nor did he pronounce them cleansed. He seems to have shied away from the prayer of these diseased men and placed their fate solely in the hands of the priests.

However, the continuation of the passage shows that this was not the reality. Jesus was not demurring from action. As they went their way and before they had reached the priests, the lepers found that they were healed. Thus,

Jesus had intervened, but in a manner so discreet that Luke doesn't spend any time describing how.

It was certainly the case that Jesus respected the Law and that he made sure it was respected by the ten lepers; therefore they were to go, as required by the Law, to expose their condition to the priests, who were the only parties accredited to confirm their healing.

The mystery of the healing

"As they were going, it came to pass that they were healed," Luke tells us. This is where the miracle is! It imposes itself upon us, but without actually being described. "It came to pass . . ." Luke leaves things vague. A miracle is always a miracle; it is to be pondered, not appropriated!

Luke preserves the sense of mystery by mentioning the healing of the lepers only after they depart from Jesus, with a slight delay: "As they were going." It was along the way, after leaving, that the lepers discovered themselves to be healed. Jesus' entourage didn't witness a thing![3] It was not for his followers' benefit that Jesus did the miracle, not for show; it was for the lepers alone, those who were truly interested in the substance of the miracle. What humility! What humble love for these outcasts!

The mystery is also maintained in Luke's choice of grammatical construction with the verb "cleanse." He uses the verb in the passive, the well-known passive which Biblicists refer to as the "divine passive."

"They were cleansed," we are told. We have just affirmed that Jesus cleansed these men, but in doing so I

3. There were people around. Jesus was speaking to witnesses in vv 17 and 18, where he speaks of the Samaritan in the third person. However, the connection between Jesus and these witnesses is so discreet that Luke does not specify whom he was addressing.

may have spoken a little too quickly! What do we know in fact? Jesus had simply sent them away, without any other intervention. We should limit ourselves to what Luke says with his divine passive. This mode of expression allows what God has done to be stated, but without naming him. Who then, really, cleansed these men along the way if not God? It is he alone who heals leprosy.

Out of respect for the holiness of God, Israel avoided at all costs pronouncing his name, precisely because it was a name of such purity that it would only be defiled if spoken by impure lips. The divine passive is particularly precious because it allows us to name the unnameable. Every reader who is sensitive to this Jewish preoccupation understands that "they were cleansed" means "they were cleansed by God." Luke has no need to be explicit; everything is clear. God had intervened . . .

However the passage is so constructed that this divine passive also invites a different reading. The lepers spoke to Jesus, not God, because they couldn't pray to God. Given that the healing was granted them, it would seem indeed that the author of the miracle must be Jesus himself. The turn of phrase therefore invites us to understand, "They were healed by Jesus."

This is the quandary in which Luke places us by the vague way in which he recounts the healing: was it God who intervened or was it Jesus? At the very least, and this perhaps is what Luke suggests, in the end, might it not be both of them? The proximity between Jesus and God is so close . . . would Jesus himself be God? This is very sensitively-expressed in Luke; in the way he reports the miracle he opens the text up to the inexpressible, and immerses our faith in mystery: "As they were going, it came to pass that they were cleansed . . ."

Christ looks

Did Jesus then take part directly in this miracle? Certainly, but as he did so, it was with an extreme and humble discretion. It was not by the words he spoke, "Go and show yourselves to the priests." Such words are not the cause of a miracle! Neither did Jesus intervene in terms of an action, as was the case with the other leper, whom he had touched (Luke 5:13).

In Luke's Gospel, mention is often made of the way people sought to touch Jesus because power went out of him (cf. 6:19, 8:46). Here there was no physical contact with Jesus.

How, then, did Jesus' intervention take place? It is here that the attentive reader suddenly becomes aware of a wonderful detail in the text. Luke in fact carefully tells us that before he spoke to the lepers, Jesus "looked" at them. The look of Jesus . . . ! Is a look from Christ able to cleanse the unclean? That is indeed what Luke seems to suggest, and this is the direction in which he points our meditation by means of this verb: "Having looked at them . . . ." Jesus sent the lepers away after fixing his gaze upon them. Christ is a person of such purity that a look from him must of necessity be perfectly pure. Anyone who meets his gaze could indeed by cleansed . . . Only the painters of icons are able to convey the unspeakably pure nature of Jesus' gaze, so pure as to purify the person on whom it is fixed . . .

Jesus had no need to touch the lepers; it was enough for him to look at them! These men, as they turned away, could go and show themselves to the priests; in Jesus they had met with a look from God! They knew themselves to have been cleansed! The miracle had sprung from the purifying power of a look, and the lives of these men were transformed; they were clean . . .

The act of thanksgiving

While the other nine proceeded on their way to the priests as the Law required, one of the lepers turned back on his tracks, giving praise. As Luke puts it, he "glorified God in a loud voice" (v.15), showing clearly that the man was not mistaken about what had happened; it was God who was responsible.

Nevertheless, Luke adds, the leper, even as he glorified God, fell at the feet of Jesus and addressed his thanksgiving to him: "He gave *him* thanks" (v 16).

At the same time, Luke says both that he gave glory "to God" and thanks "to Jesus," as if we had here two interchangeable expressions or synonyms. Isn't this simply a way of telling us that Jesus is God? It is surely the case that for the leper the miracle that gave rise to his thanksgiving came both from Jesus and from God. What point was there then in going to the priests; there was someone here greater than any priest! Was it not God himself who was present in this man from Galilee? "He fell on his face at Jesus' feet, giving thanks to him."

Jesus received this action of thanksgiving, but when he came to speak of it, he did not attribute it to himself but referred it to God: "Is there only this foreigner to be found returning to give glory *to God?*" Humbly, Jesus considered that the thanksgiving was due to his Father, not to himself!

A miracle, followed by thanksgiving; the passage might have stopped here and left us to ponder this healed and cleansed man who gives thanks, prostrated at Jesus feet. Nevertheless the account keeps moving, due to a simple detail hitherto left in the shadows by the evangelist: "Now, this man was a Samaritan."

The man was a Samaritan

A man had been healed, cleansed of leprosy. For him it was a day of deepest thankfulness towards the one who had opened the door to a new life. The future lay before him; only there was this, that the man was a Samaritan. Up to this point this was not something we knew, but now we learn it, and it tells us that we are in the presence of someone notoriously unclean! In fact, sick or not, leprous or not, in Israel's eyes a Samaritan was certainly unclean, congenitally so! This man on his face before Jesus was healed, cleansed of his leprosy, but not cleansed of his membership of the Samaritan people. Even healed, for Israel he was still a foreigner; and the Law was definite – every foreigner was unclean to such a degree that if he were to approach the sanctuary, he was to be put to death (Num 1:51; 3:38).

The issue of impurity is not now governed by the question of the leprosy but a question of identity. It is this that is taken up in the renewal of the account, leading us deeper into the question of impurity. It picks up and will conclude with a very strong word, not yet used: not "healed," not "cleansed," but "saved."[4] This verb "to save" says something more, something of which the nine other lepers were not to be beneficiaries. All ten were healed and cleansed, certainly, but only one is saved.

In this second section of the account there is a new word from Jesus, corresponding to a new intervention, a second miracle, no longer the miracle of healing, but the miracle of salvation. This second intervention of Jesus is presented as a response to the actions of the Samaritan, the response to an unformulated request which is nonetheless heard by Jesus

4. In the Greek, three distinct verbs: *katharizo, iomai* and *sozo*. (Trans.)

and which it is now our turn to understand too. Where in the text do we find this desire of the Samaritan for a second intervention by Jesus?

A paradoxical attitude

When he comes before Jesus, the Samaritan gives thanks for his healing, but his attitude is nevertheless unusual. When we give thanks, as a rule the correct thing is to stand up straight and lift our eyes to heaven. Thus, for example, we see Jesus lift his eyes upwards before Lazarus' tomb as he gave thanks (John 11:41). But here, as he gives thanks, the Samaritan is not standing; he is on his face: "He fell on his face at Jesus' feet."

This "prostration" is not an attitude for giving thanks but for supplication, as we see again with Jesus, for example, when, as he pleaded with God in Gethsemane, "he fell on his face" (Matt 26:39).

In Luke's Gospel too, it is quite clear: those who "fall on their face" are in an attitude of request, of supplication (cf. 5:12). The same applies to anyone who falls to their knees (5:8) or at Jesus' feet (8:28, 41, 47): Simon Peter, a leper, the demoniac, Jairus, the woman with the haemorrhage, all of them, when they were on their faces, were pleading.

What then is the meaning of the attitude of this Samaritan who bows down as he gives thanks? I believe, quite simply, that he is both pleading and giving thanks, that he is pleading for one thing and giving thanks for another. He is giving thanks for his healing, but in falling down he is asking something else of Jesus.

Joy and sorrow

We often have difficulty imagining it possible to give thanks and to petition at the same time; this is above all true in western Churches in which rational logic dominates and almost requires us to categorize. I belong to a church in which the prayers are often quite distinct; there are prayers for giving thanks, and others for petition. The Sunday liturgy of the Reformed Church of France is remarkably structured in this way; there is a time for supplication, and a time for praise.

Putting things in categories like this is pedagogically fine, but biblical logic doesn't seem to be so simple! Thus, in the book of Psalms, for example, the greater part of the psalms of petition are often also psalms of praise (as Ps 22), and the psalms of praise also contain petitions (Ps 9)! Joy and sorrow are intermingled in this way. This mingling goes as far as the Psalmist saying, "Even as I cried out to you, praise was already on my tongue" (66:17).

We have to submit ourselves to the evidence: the human heart can be the place of both petition and thanksgiving at the same time, and prayer can express this apparent contradiction, containing both complaint and thanks; in the end this is how it should be, and it is a thing of beauty.

Johann Sebastian Bach, though protestant and western, understood this remarkably well, as demonstrated in his wonderful chorale, "Jesu, joy of man's desiring."[5] The well-known counterpoint of this chorale is all in triplets and sounds like a dance in its deep and continuous joy. It is superb! Then, even more superb, above the counterpoint in the instruments, the *cantus firmus*, the chorale itself, comes in, composed of slow, weighty phrases, with words expressing extraordinary supplication. The piece wonderfully combines the two elements. Bach, a true man

5. Jesus bleibet meine Freude. BMV 147 (Trans.)

of prayer, understood the complexity of the human attitude before God.

Continuing with the Old Testament, there is a Hebrew verb (*ranan*) which has two distinct meanings which seem at first irreconcilable. It means "cry for joy" (Ps 5:12) and "cry in distress" (Lam 2:19)! Both meanings! The word *rinnah*, which is derived from it, is found in prayer both to give thanks to God (Ps 105:43) and in supplication (1 Kgs 8:28). There is no way to produce in one word a translation with both Hebrew aspects. Translators are therefore obliged to choose one of the two meanings according to context. It is much better if we can understand that mixed in with the prayer of supplication there is true joy, and that with the thanksgiving there is also real supplication. What does this have to say to us?

Anyone who pleads with God because of their sin, their uncleanness or some other misery, cries out in distress, but they do so in the joy of being able, despite everything, to address their prayer to God, in the joy of knowing that the prayer is heard. It is in fact wonderful to be able to bring our pleadings to God! It is a source of real joy! As well as this, a person who expresses joy to God over some benefit that has been received also knows how unworthy they are of such great blessing, unworthy indeed of any sign of consideration on God's part; it is impossible to express the joy without including the petition linked to the unworthiness. Further, when we express our joy to God, we also in some form petition him to enable the joy to remain . . .

When Job was knocked over by the avalanche of disasters that engulfed him, he took the attitude of a suppliant: "He rent his garments, shaved his head, and threw himself on the ground"; in this attitude of deep mourning he cried out, "Blessed be the name of the Lord!" (1:20–21). In this act of suppliant thanksgiving we find the paradoxical and profound truth of faith.

When a monk pronounces a doxology as thanksgiving, he doesn't do so with his eyes lifted up to heaven, but bowed down, in supplication . . .

The prayer of the heart, dear to the orthodox, contains both thanksgiving ("Lord Jesus Christ, Son of God") and supplication ("Have mercy on me, a sinner").

When anyone stands before God, Luther said, they are both righteous and a penitent sinner,[6] so much so that their repentance mixes thanksgiving for pardon with the sinners supplication.

The unstated plea

What, then, was the Samaritan doing at Jesus' feet? His thanksgiving poses us no problem because it flows from the miraculous healing and cleansing of his leprosy. Also though, bowed down before his Savior, his attitude has an unstated plea which Jesus understands and to which he is able to respond: "Go, your faith has saved you." What was it he asked of Jesus by this prostration, and what did he obtain in the salvation granted him?

I believe that he was asking for a second cleansing, no longer for his leprosy, which he had already obtained and for which he was giving thanks, but for his heart, the internal cleansing of his deeper self; he, the Samaritan, was particularly concerned about this, a congenitally unclean person in the eyes of Israel; he found himself in the presence of a Galilean before whom he knew himself to be fundamentally unclean.

---

6. Simul justus et peccator, comprehensor et viator. (Trans.)

Not only must he have still felt unclean in himself by the simple fact of meeting a Galilean, but he was also sensitive because of his knowledge of the Law on leprosy. The Law, in fact, contains a lengthy chapter about the purification of lepers (Lev 14); it becomes clear that this purification concerns firstly the disease itself, the cleansing of the skin, but then, secondly, the inner impurity within the heart. Cleansing of the heart is not a Christian invention; it was already clearly present in the Torah, and the Samaritan was perfectly informed of this. The salvation granted by Jesus therefore includes the healing of the leprosy and the cleansing of the heart. We will examine the law . . .

The purification of lepers

In Leviticus 14, in the first twenty verses, we find the description of a ritual spread across eight days, consisting of three separate stages, each of which ends with the conclusion: "He is clean" (vv 8, 9 and 20). As each stage is concluded, the next step is not a repetition of the same act of purification; there are three different, successive cleansings which enter deeper and deeper into the being. The first has to do with the external cleansing of the leprosy and the renewal of relations with those who were healthy; the other two concern inner cleansing for the renewal of relations with the close family, and then with God.

The first cleansing was obtained at the end of the first day (v 8), the second on the seventh day (v 9) and the last on the eighth day (v 10). At the end of the first cleansing, the healed leper could enter the camp but not his tent. At the end of the second, he could enter his tent, but not the sanctuary. At the close of the third, he now finally regained access to the holy place (v 11).

The law therefore sets out a clearly marked gradation of cleansing. Firstly, the healed and cleansed leper was sufficiently clean to rejoin society. Clean as he was in others' eyes, he was not yet clean enough for his close family, for his wife and children, as specified in the Neophyte Targum: "He is to stay outside the tent where he lives and is not to approach his wife" (14:8). The closer he is to someone else and the stronger the bonds, the deeper the degree of cleansing must be. One might be clean in the eyes of others, whoever they might be, but not in the eyes of those closest, those with whom each day is shared. Better than anyone, our intimate relations really know what is in our heart. This is a particularly important fact, confirmed by experience. Those near us see most deeply into our hearts and know how relative is our apparent purity, and the extent to which it hides impurities which cannot escape their eyes.

While the first cleansing took just one day, the cleansing to rejoin one's intimates required seven! Seven long days in which nothing happened — except for deep examination of the heart in the light of prayer . . .

The eighth day

Next, even though now clean with regard to family, the man was still unclean when it came to God; a further, much deeper purification was needed. A person who is clean in the eyes of those close to him is still unclean in God's eyes, God, who is the most intimate of intimates! God sees what no person can see, into the deepest reaches of our hearts.

The outward cleansing of the leprosy, allowing the man back into society, was obtained on the first day, but when it came to those closest, the cleansing required much more, seven entire days. Cleansing with regard to God is so deep that it can only take place on the eighth day, which is to say on a day which does not belong to the normal week, a day which overflows from the week and which is difficult to fit in with our way of apportioning of time, a day without evening or morning, outside of time and yet within it, belonging in a way to eternity . . . No doubt a lengthy journey through life is necessary, perhaps a whole life, with one foot already in eternity, if we are to truly be pure in God's eyes.

On the eighth day, the priest performed an extended ritual, but it is interesting to note that the leper did nothing. He no longer had to wash himself or his clothes, as had been the case on the first and seventh days (vv 8 and 9.) This is a way of saying that the leper has no power to do anything to the deepest places within, where the uncleanness lies, and that the cleansing pertains to God alone, through the medium of the animal sacrifices performed by the priest. The leper was entirely dependent on God's intervention.

God alone can cleanse, yes, but all the same we should note that the leper, even though he does nothing, is there at the entrance to the sanctuary. His part is to be sure to be there (14:11). The only, but essential, way in which he participates is to approach the sanctuary with an offering, and in this way to open himself to God; to experience in his heart, in his silent prayer, the purpose for which the sacrifices are offered. He no longer needs to wash himself or his garments, but he does need to open his heart to the one who alone can cleanse it. The whole matter is this opening of the heart to God . . .

The very moment in the ritual with the greatest accent on inner cleansing is also the moment when the importance of the body is most strongly underlined. On the eighth day, the priest put the sacrificial blood on the lobe of the right ear, on the right thumb, and on the right big toe of the person being cleansed, then he repeated this act with oil, and also put some of this on the man's head; inner cleansing does not imply that the body is now left behind, but indeed and undoubtedly, the very reverse! The purer a person is inwardly, the more this shines through in the flesh, in the features of the face . . .

The earlobe, the thumb and the big toe . . . curiously the ceremony for the cleansing of the leper is very close to that for the investiture of a priest (Exod 29:20); the cleansing of a person who has known what it is to be a leper allows him full access to God such as only a priest enjoys as he enters the holy of holies . . .

The cleansing the Samaritan requests of Jesus, after obtaining cleansing for his leprosy, is the double inner cleansing of the seventh and eighth days, which only God, in the end, can perform.

The Samaritan is there, on his face before Jesus, his heart open to him. Confronted by this mute plea, Jesus replies simply and sovereignly, "Stand up and go; your faith has saved you."

The closer God approaches

It is never stated in Leviticus 14 that God cleanses! Nevertheless, it is surely he and he alone who is able to cleanse the heart to its very depths. The Law states that the leper "purifies himself" by his following of the ritual (14:4, 7, 8, 11, 14, 17, 18, 19). It is also stated that the priest purifies him (14:11), but never that God does so! In the ritual, God is not the subject of any verb at all, and it seems as though he is inactive. The reality though must be that he is very active, but this is not stated because it is beyond expression. God is at work as he alone is able, in a way which we are unable to describe. No one knows how

God cleanses, but nevertheless the fact is there, very real. The last word of the ritual clearly states of the man who is standing at the entrance to the sanctuary that "he is clean." The cleansing is there, so deep that it could only come from God . . . Nothing is said as to what God does, but it all takes place in his presence, "before his face," as the text specifies (v 11), which is to say, with him looking on, under his supervision . . .

Things are just the same here with Jesus. His gaze alone had cleansed the ten lepers of their disease; the Samaritan then returned and fell on his face before Jesus, simply opening himself anew to his scrutiny . . .

On the first day of his cleansing, the leper took part in the ritual by washing himself, shaving, and washing his clothing (v 8). On the seventh day he did the same again (v 9). But the eighth day he no longer bathed, shaved, or washed his clothing. There was nothing more he could do; he could only move in God's direction since God was beyond his reach. Everything was to take place in the depths of the heart, where no person can do anything except open up to God and allow him to mysteriously accomplish his work of cleansing through the actions performed by the priest.

In God's eyes, the impurity is so deep that he alone is able to intervene. A beautiful example of this is given in the experience of Isaiah on the day he saw the majesty of God in the Temple (Isa 6). This event did indeed take place in the Temple; this means that, since Isaiah was in the sanctuary, he was ritually clean having rigorously followed all the regulations for cleansing. Then, when God appeared to him and so drew much closer, Isaiah, although "pure," cried out, "Woe is me, I am lost, for I am a man of unclean lips!" (6:5) What could be the cause of this sudden awareness of impurity in a ritually clean man except the nearness of

God? The closer God draws, the more unclean we feel, with an impurity so deep that an entire life would be needed to be washed clean.

What ritual was Isaiah to follow? None, because there was nothing further prescribed in the Law than what he had already performed! It was then that a seraphim came to him and did what he could never do himself: he took a burning coal from the altar with tongs and touched the prophet's lips, thus purifying him. Through his seraphim intermediary, God himself drew near and touched the man. Nothing unclean can approach God, but the miracle is that God approaches whatever is unclean so that it may be cleansed! This wonderful grace of God steps over the obstacle and accomplishes the impossible . . .

The impurity of sins

What is the source of inner impurity? Not of the leprosy, which was already healed, but of the sins? Standing in front of the sanctuary, before God, the impurity became apparent; this is why it was only on the eighth day, not before, that there was the issue of the three sacrifices, one as an expiation of voluntary sins, another for involuntary sins, and the third, a burnt offering of thanksgiving. It was only at this moment, when the man stood before the sanctuary, before the house of God, that he became aware of his sins as a sort of inner leprosy of which he needed to be cleansed.

The sins of which the leper was cleansed might have lain behind his leprosy, though this is not necessarily so. At times the leprosy might originate in a sin, as in the case of Gehazi (2 Kgs 5:26-27), or Miriam (Num 12:1-10). In Gehazi's case the sin was theft, and in Miriam's slander, but this is exceptional. Israel did not systematically present leprosy as punishment for some sin; when the priest diagnosed the disease, as in Leviticus 13, no issue was made of sin.

The sins of which the leper was to be cleansed are the sins committed while he was diseased, those of which he could not by cleansed by the prescribed forms of worship, excluded as he was by his disease from any access to the Temple and participation in the penitential rituals. Once healed, the leper, in his return to the Temple, could finally fulfill the prescriptions of the Law for the cleansing of sins.

If, as we have said, impurity was not just at a moral level but had to do with relationship with others and with God, the same is true of sins. A sin is a closing off, a rejection of the other or of God, an inner leprosy.

We see that if the inner impurity is tied to sin, then we are all involved in this impurity, whether leprous or not. How true this is! In God's eyes, we are all people of an unclean heart.

Speaking directly to this, Jesus, for our benefit, makes wonderfully and decisively clear what brings about a person's impurity.

Jesus and physical impurity

One particular day, when the disciples ate without washing their hands, the Pharisees, those experts in questions of purity, remarked on this to Jesus; he reacted in a very significant manner, in two ways (Mark 7). A person's impurity, he says firstly, does not come from the outside, from foods, for example, which might make him unclean. There was therefore no necessity to wash the hands!

With comments like this, Jesus reversed all the laws of purification that said that impurity is received from the exterior, by contact. Jesus' attitude here, as its meaning was pursued, helped the Church free itself of this concept of impurity. Thus, Jesus was free to touch a leper (Luke 5:13), a dead man (8:54), or allow himself to be touched by a woman with a haemorrhage (8:44), each of which otherwise represented notorious sources of external impurity. Not only in each of these cases did Jesus not become unclean, but, and this was the first time such a thing had happened in the entire history of Israel, the unclean were cleansed. No one other than God could so turn things around in Israel; and Jesus, as God, did what God alone can do . . .

Since that time it has been granted to Christians to benefit from this freedom received in Christ. In Christ we can touch a leper, a dead body or any physically impure person without ourselves becoming impure. Thanks to Christ there has been a true revolution which frees us and enables us to transmit the cleansing received from Christ. To bless the dead by laying hands on the body is no longer a defilement, but on the contrary, I believe, a cleansing.

Impure thoughts

This freedom with regard to physical impurity is a wonderful gift of God, and no doubt we fail to appreciate it sufficiently! However, what Jesus said about impurity does not stop here but has another aspect, and we are not always attentive to this either. While what he says is certainly liberating when it comes to the physical, he also turns things around in another way and we need to consider this. In Jesus' eyes, not all uncleanness was done away with in this way — there remains impurity of heart, the inner impurity which is so important that it defiles a person completely. As he said to the disciples: "That which comes out of a person is what defiles them. It is from within, from the human heart, that evil thoughts issue: adulteries, immoralities, murders, theft, covetousness, wickedness, fraud, licentiousness, the evil eye, slander, pride, foolishness. All these evil things come from within and defile a man" (Mark 7:20-23).

If Jesus enumerated the types of impurity within the heart at such length, it must have been to draw the disciples' attention to the way it concerned them, and to the importance and seriousness of inner impurity.

The list is shorter in Matthew, but the two lists have in common that they start with the mention of "evil thoughts" (Mark 7:20, Matt 15:19). The words that follow in reality do no more than detail what is contained in the first expression, listing possible thoughts.

Evil thoughts are what make a person unclean. What Jesus is saying here speaks to all of us. What does leprosy matter, or other external causes of impurity? What matters and concerns each of us are the thoughts; not all the thoughts, because there are pure thoughts, but the impure thoughts. The Fathers saw clearly that Jesus was giving no more than a sample in the list transmitted by Mark, lengthy though it is. Impure thoughts are numerous, of great variety, and more or less deeply rooted in humanity, right down to the pride which is without doubt the deepest impurity; Jesus places it last on his list, together with the mental troubles that stem from it. The list, as reported by Mark, seems to move from the more superficial to the deepest. Pride, and the foolishness associated with it are, before God, the impurities requiring the greatest attention.

"Blessed are the pure in heart," marvels Jesus. Their inward eye is so pure that they see God! But it is so rare, a true gift of God! A miracle!

The awareness of impure thoughts is not a Christian invention or an innovation of Jesus. It was already an issue in the Old Testament. Impure thoughts are the central focus of Job, for example: when his children got together for a feast, he had the custom of offering a sacrifice the next day for each of them, saying to himself, "It may be that my sons have sinned and offended God in their hearts" (Job 1:5). Job, full of tact, didn't ask his children anything about the thoughts of their hearts, but he was so concerned that he offered sacrifices so that God would, if necessary, pardon and cleanse the hearts defiled by impure thoughts.

Psalm 24, furthermore, is also very explicit. "Who can enter the sanctuary?" it asks. Not, it replies, the person who is outwardly, ritually pure, but "the one who has . . . a pure heart" (v 4). The psalmist was thoroughly aware of the inner reality, that the heart can be pure or impure.

Jesus enables us to go a step further, underlining emphatically the way an impure thought can defile a person's whole being.

When we speak of "impure thoughts," we are often inclined these days to suppose that the issue here is only thoughts of a sexual nature; but Jesus' list is much more extensive — slander, evil speaking, jealousy, pride, contempt, covetousness, fraud . . . these are what defile, often much more deeply than the thought of adultery.

If I should judge and condemn someone in my heart, even with the other person knowing nothing of it, the judgmental thought defiles me inwardly, and falsifies my ensuing attitude towards that person. When I close my heart to another with thoughts that run them down, that disdain or despise, all of this defiles me inwardly. When I covet the goods or the wife of my neighbor, though only in my heart, again, this is an inner defilement.

When Jesus washed the feet of his disciples, and declared that one of them was unclean while the others were not (John 13:10), the issue was inner impurity. Judas in fact was unclean because he had unclean thoughts within, diverse and mixed up no doubt, but certainly not sexual. Judas' unclean thoughts meant that he couldn't continue in company with the others or with Jesus. "He quickly left," John tells us, and adds carefully, "it was night" (13:30). In the darkness of the night, Judas found himself alone, cut off from others and from the Lord Jesus. His impure thoughts made him an outcast. This is the truth about inner impurity — an inner leprosy which turns us into exiles.

Self mastery

We have a great number of thoughts within us; some are pure, others are not, according to whether or not they are inclined towards God and his will. In itself, a thought is neither pure nor impure; it becomes one or the other according to what or to whom it is directed. The issue is less one of morality than of attitude before God. A loving thought is pure when it orientates the heart towards God or one's neighbor. It becomes impure when it alienates from God or is mixed with covetousness, jealousy, the desire to control, the thirst to possess, vainglory, or anything else that spoils a righteous attitude before God.

Our place is to know how to direct our thoughts, to dominate them and not allow them to dominate us. This is self-control, a magnificent virtue; and we well know, reader friend, how difficult it is!

Of ourselves, none of us manages to master our own thoughts; there is a constant need of God's help. Paul had good reason to say that self-control is a fruit of the Holy Spirit (Gal 5:23). Without the help of the Holy Spirit, we do not know how to master our thoughts; we don't know how to see to it that they are directed towards right relations with others and God. "Without me you can do nothing," Jesus adds (15:5). This too is true: without Christ, without the Holy Spirit, we do not know how to master our own thoughts, and every effort in the inner life is vain.

"Watch over your heart," says the book of Proverbs (4:23). This indeed is where self-mastery begins. Vigilance is the first priority. Be attentive to every thought that presents itself to your heart and drive away with all speed everything which is impure. The whole spiritual life, every act of discipline, consists of inner vigilance and the struggle against impure thoughts. It requires care, the effort of each moment, with the constant help of God.

What are we to do, though, when our vigilance fails and the struggle ends in a setback? What are we to do when our heart has been soiled by some impure thought which through our negligence has found a home within us? How are we to purify ourselves? What ritual are we to follow for the cleansing of the heart? Only God can cleanse the heart; our part is therefore to turn humbly to him, open ourselves up to him and seek cleansing from him. Later we will see how God undertakes our cleansing, but before the request for God's intervention, we should pause a little over the seriousness of inner impurity.

Maximus the Confessor says that impurity will cost us any closeness with God! It is that serious! Maximus was right: the impurity of our soul places the heart in such darkness that we become incapable of perceiving God's presence. If our inner eye is impure we can see nothing of God. If our ears are impure they will hear nothing from God. If our taste is impure, it is no longer possible to taste the goodness of the Lord. The whole being is defiled by the impure thoughts of the heart, says Jesus! We need to recognize clearly that we are so habituated to our inner impurity that we wind up accommodating it . . . "Woe is me!"

The seriousness of impurity

While it's true that both the Law of God and human laws punish any faults committed, there is no law, not even God's, which punishes impure thoughts. Does this mean this sort of impurity is not a serious matter? We should not too quickly suppose that serious consequences relate only to legal penalties. There are so many other outworkings which do not concern the law; we might begin as an example with sickness . . .

Jesus underlines the seriousness of impure thoughts in a well-known passage from the Sermon on the Mount: "Whoever looks at a woman and lusts after her has already committed adultery with her in his heart" (Matt 5:28). It is certainly true that this kind of adultery is not punishable by Law since there is no victim; there is no witness either! No one can bring a complaint! There is no effective adultery . . . so what is the point of all the fuss . . . ?

When Jesus denounces this adultery it is because it defiles the heart of the one who commits it. The victim is the person whose heart is defiled. Anyone whose heart is defiled is defiled in their whole being; we know this attack on our being to be as serious as an inner leprosy, even if no one else knows a thing, and though there is no law to impose a sanction. A person who is inwardly diseased goes in search of a doctor, not a judge. Therefore we need to turn to God the healer, and entrust to him the care of our spiritual life, seriously affected and perturbed as it is by inner impurity.

The serious import of the inner defilement is that it affects everything in our heart, and this, according to the Bible, means the whole spiritual life, our ability to love, to be sure, but also our faith, our spiritual understanding, our prayer . . . Since the whole spiritual life has its source in the heart, everything is defiled when the heart is impure.

Impure prayer

How many times has my prayer been disturbed, interrupted, distracted by impure thoughts? I wouldn't know where to begin! I do know that such thoughts defile my prayer.

Of course impure thoughts are not only those of a sexual nature; these are among them but are far from the only ones! The thoughts that defile prayer include resentment, anger, vengeance, disdain, jealousy . . . all of these disturb, falsify and pollute our perception of others and of God.

A good example is given by Jesus himself in the well-known parable of the Pharisee and the publican (Luke 18:9-14). The two men go up to the Temple to pray. The Pharisee, who is so attentive to all the rituals of purification, has most certainly done everything necessary to enter the Temple pure. We see this ritually clean man exposing his spiritual life to God, a really honorable spiritual life at that! He fasts twice a week and gives the tenth of all his goods. He thanks God for all this, but with such a spirit of superiority as to reveal the substantial pride of his heart. "O God, I give you thanks that I am not as other men, extortioners, unjust, adulterers . . . ." Pride defiles his heart.

The prayer which issues from his heart is unclean, and in no way acceptable to God.

However ritually pure, he was a man who had become entirely impure, the reverse of the publican; this man might well have had his hands soiled by the money he handled every day in his profession, but his heart was made pure by his humility. "Standing at a distance, he dared not raise up his eyes to heaven; instead, beating his breast, he said, "O God, be propitious to me, a sinner." The publican's relation to money was external to his humble heart. A humble heart that opens itself up to God is purified since the humility comes from God. The prayer that issues from it is pure.

Pure prayer is prayer undamaged by any impure thought. Happy are the pure in heart because their pure prayer rises up to God, who receives it favorably.

What comes out of the heart, this is what defiles the whole man, says Jesus! Pride defiled not only the Pharisee's prayer but the whole of his person, his whole life, every activity, his entire being, right to the very last ounce of who he was! This is to say that the rest of his spiritual life was also defiled. The fasting he practiced so diligently out of faithfulness to the Law was defiled by his pride. The tithe he gave so scrupulously out of respect for the Law was defiled by his pride. Pride defiles every discipline, every performance of the commandments. Pride is a real internal leprosy corrupting all relations with God and with others . . . ! One simple prideful thought and everything is corrupted, like a perfume of great price into which a fly has fallen!

God alone is able to purify the heart, while pride closes the heart against God with the pretension of being able to purify itself without God's help. Humility by contrast, opens the heart to God to be purified by him. God never forces the door of the heart, but knocks, and calls for humility. By falling at Jesus' feet, the Samaritan was humbly opening his heart and waiting for the Lord to perform his work.

Pure love

Love springs from the heart, but if the heart is unclean, then its love is too. It is a good thing to love one's neighbor, but it is also important to question the quality of this love. Is it pure or impure? Impure love is a love which is inhabited and defiled by impure thoughts, by thoughts of adultery for example, but also the thought of captivating, enslaving, or shining in the eyes of others, the desire to profit from a neighbor, to have some hold over him, to be honored by him . . . and isn't this so often the case in the final account? Love of neighbor and of God are defiled by other loves which spoil and pollute: the love of money, the love of glory, the love of power . . . Impure love defiles relations with others like an inner leprosy. Again, purification is not an end in itself but a necessary passage to the reestablishment of true relations with others and with God.

What then is pure love in a pure heart?

There is only one truly pure love, God's! A pure heart is the fruit of God's working, of God, who comes to purify by his own love, in synergy with the human effort to fight against every impurity. It is a heart which loves with a love transformed by God, a love humble enough to allow God to introduce his own love and turn it into a divine-human love. When we know ourselves to be loved by the pure love of another, isn't it the case that we discover in this something of God's love for us?

The pure heart is so humble that it doesn't have the feeling of holding the love of God, but others will perceive it and give thanks to God; through the medium of such a heart they receive something of the divine love.

A pure mind

The human mind or intelligence also has its seat in the heart — according to Biblical thought — not in the head as we think these days. If the heart is unclean, then the mind is too. When the mind is impure it becomes unfeeling, and our understanding of God, of others and of ourselves is blighted. This speaks particularly strongly to me as a theologian, a person with a responsibility to speak truthfully about God, but the fact is that are we are all concerned with this issue from the moment we endeavor to understand our lives with others and with God. What value is there to our theology if our understanding of God and others is rendered suspect, polluted by our unclean heart?

Jesus unfailingly drew this to the attention of the theologians of his time, the Pharisees and other doctors of the Law. By describing them as hypocrites, Jesus was continually pointing out that their apparent purity was hiding a defiled heart. For Jesus, the inner impurity meant the Pharisees were particularly blind (cf. Matt 23:26–35, John 9) and equally insensitive; they were lacking in understanding (Matt 23:17) to such a degree that in their brutishness they had come to concentrate on details and overlook the core issues: "Woe unto you, scribes and Pharisees, hypocrites; you pay the tithe of mint, anise and cumin and abandon the essence of the Law, justice, mercy and faith! You should have done the one, without neglecting the rest. Blind guides, who strain at a gnat and swallow a camel!" (Matt 23:23-24).

Every defiled heart eventually produces a foolish theology. We should not, however, suppose that this concerns the Pharisees alone; the disciples themselves emerge from the gospels as being just as seriously affected. The disciples, and not the least of them, show themselves to be similarly insensitive to what lies at the heart of the Gospel, the very mystery of the person of Jesus.

The disciples' lack of understanding

When Jesus announced to his disciples that he had to die and rise again, he was exposing them to what lay at the core of his mission, the central feature of the work he had to accomplish. The Gospels tell us that when Jesus said this to the disciples, they didn't understand, and to such an extent that he had to say the same thing three times; even then it was in vain — the disciples still didn't get it! "The disciples did not understand what he was saying," Mark deplores (9:32).

What was the source of their incomprehension? Had Jesus been particularly complicated in his explanation? Not at all! Every word was perfectly simple (be handed over, suffer, die . . .) and the very word "resurrection" was in common use in Israel at the time. The word was the subject of lengthy debates between the Pharisees and Sadducees, but it was understood by all, part of the way of thinking.

What was going on then? If the words Jesus used were not complicated for the disciples, it must be that their minds were darkened so that they could not understand what Jesus was saying though it was at the very heart of his life and teaching! Where did this dullness come from? Quite simply, from their impure hearts!

As we re-read the Gospel, things become clear. It was after the second announcement of the Passion that Mark states "the disciples did not understand this saying." Immediately after this he tells us that Jesus questioned them as to what was in their hearts. Their response is then given us without any equivocation — "they were silent because along the way they had been arguing amongst themselves as to who was the greatest"! (9:34)

This is what made the disciples so lacking — their prideful thoughts! The heart defiled by pride made the disciples insensitive to the very mystery of Christ . . . How could they possibly understand Christ, the Humble in heart, when their hearts were proud? Pride has never understood humility and never will! In so far as a disciple is prideful he cannot enter into the mystery of Christ who is nothing but humility!

After the third announcement of the Passion (Mark 10:33), the disciples still didn't understand, and the continuation of the account is again just as clear: the disciples were preoccupied with a request addressed to Jesus by two of their number, and that not by the least important of them but by James and John. Their request is very indicative of the state of their hearts, the desire to sit enthroned in the best places, on the right and the left of Jesus! (10:37) Pride is the ever-present! Their hearts, even those of James and John, were unclean, stupefied by pride; they were unable to understand the humble way of the Lord's cross.

I have left till last the first announcement of the Passion; it is even clearer. On this occasion it was Peter who reacted to Jesus (Mark 8:31), resulting in the immediate reply of the Lord, "Get behind me, Satan!" (8:33). Through Peter, Satan himself was sowing into their hearts the cockleburs of impure thought. It was pride that led Peter to "reprimand" Jesus (8:32), to correct him and dictate to him the nature of his mission!

It was not until after the cross and the resurrection that the disciples finally understood, which is to say, when the

Holy Spirit had cleansed their hearts. They then understood how the cross was the working of humility. Pride can never understand anything that is humble! Only the humility of a pure heart can understand the humble heart of Christ, and it is through the Holy Spirit that this is possible since he alone, as the apostle Paul says (1 Cor 2:10), knows the depths of God. Christ's humility of heart belongs to the deep things of God.

The day Jesus spoke about the impure thoughts that defile the heart and the entire being, the disciples did not understand. Jesus had to explain it to them, but before he did so, he alerted them to the reality of their own hearts: "Are you too so without understanding?" (Mark 7:18) Jesus was well aware of the state of his disciples' hearts!

The insistence of the Gospels on this point is there to alert us too to the reality of our impure hearts and the failure of mind that flows from it. What a poor sort of theologian I am, with my heart still so wrapped up in pride! Like any person sick with inner leprosy, we too, and me first, must throw ourselves down at the feet of Christ. "Lord Jesus Christ, Son of God, have pity on us! Cleanse my heart that I may enter into the mystery of your life, the mystery of your being."

Humble before the Humble one

When the Samaritan came to cast himself down at Jesus' feet, the disciples were present (cf. 17:5), and, as we learn from the surrounding context, the Pharisees too. It was to all of them that Jesus was speaking as he said of this man, "Is only this stranger found to return and give glory to God?" Then, in the midst of so many people of impure hearts, he said to the Samaritan, "Stand up and go your way; your faith has saved you!" If the Pharisees or the disciples with their impure hearts had spoken to this unclean Samaritan, what would they have said? It would be better not to know! What's for sure is that Jesus saw in the heart of this man a faith of such humility that he exclaimed, "Your faith has saved you!"

There is no doubt about this Samaritan's humility. The simple fact of his falling on his face, a Samaritan before a Galilean, demonstrates this clearly.

The Samaritan asked nothing of Jesus explicitly, but Jesus understood. He understood because he saw what was in the man's heart. Luke notes this in another passage: "Jesus saw the thoughts of their hearts" (9:47). Insight of great purity is necessary to see into the hearts of others in this way. This is the way Jesus saw, and this explains how just a look from him, pure as it was, could, as we noted, cleanse the ten lepers.

The Samaritan had no need to express what was in his mind; Jesus saw into his heart and understood. Jesus' heart is pure enough to hear what is not said, and to understand what is not expressed. The purity of his heart flows from his humility.

Niketas Stetathos[7] says that there is a threefold depth to humility; first there is humility of speech, the fruit of long discipline; then the humility of behavior, the result of still deeper discipline; and finally, humility of heart which comes from God alone and which purifies the heart.

The Samaritan was humble in his speech, having been able to say, with the nine others, "Have mercy on us!" He was humble in the way he bore himself, a Samaritan on his

7. 11th century Byzantine theologian, biographer of Symeon the New Theologian. (Trans.)

face before a Galilean. Was he humble of heart? I would have had no idea, but Jesus knew!

"Stand up," says Jesus. In speaking like this, Jesus implicitly recognizes the way the man had humbled himself before him; he welcomed the Samaritan's humility. Humility opens the unclean heart and welcomes cleansing, as we see in this case. This unclean man opened his heart by prostrating and abasing himself before Jesus.

Jesus didn't say, "Your humility has saved you," but, "Your faith has saved you." He speaks of faith because faith always includes humility. I am very much afraid that prideful faith is nothing but a simulation of faith! A proud person reposes no confidence in anyone other than himself.

That Jesus was humble is clearly apparent in what he said to the Samaritan. "Your faith has saved you," he says. Jesus spoke like this out of humility. It is evident to the Samaritan, as to the disciples, that it was Jesus who had saved him, as he had saved so many other sick people. In all the Gospels, Jesus never said, "I have saved you." This is his humility. "Your faith has saved you," he says, underlining the high standing of the other and never pushing himself forward. It would be humble of anyone who hears this phrase of Jesus' to reply, "It is you who have saved me and not my faith!"

Is there only this stranger?

The Samaritan, bowed down before Jesus, knew himself to be inwardly unclean, as deeply unclean as any Samaritan would be when dealing with a Galilean. He knew his prayer was impure and did not so much as dare to pray out loud in the Lord's presence. Nevertheless, Jesus perceived something else in him, a profound but silent groaning which touched him.

Jesus spoke a most important word that should attract our attention, though it might also cause confusion: "This stranger"!

For an Israelite, a Samaritan was a vulgar stranger, a heretic, notoriously unclean. In the mouth of Jesus of Nazareth, a Galilean, as in the mouth of any other Jew, the word "stranger" to describe the Samaritan at his feet might have been charged with a degree of condescending disdain and even contempt: "Is there no one but this stranger ... !"

But that is not at all what Jesus was saying; indeed he was praising the man's faith. In fact, Christ was careful to use a word whose meaning we need to consider.

The usual word in Greek for stranger is *"xenos"*; this is the word found everywhere and it is more or less instinct with contempt. It is the word used throughout the New Testament, save just once only ... and that is right here!

Jesus used another word, one with nothing of contempt about it, but rather, admiration. This word in Greek is *allogenes*; we do also translate this as "stranger", but it means more exactly "a person who is born differently, of another birth." When Jesus says this, the word surely connotes something he said elsewhere, in his dialogue with Nicodemus (John 3), about the new birth, the birth from above, the birth in the Spirit of holiness, the birth which overrides every congenital impurity since in the Spirit there is neither Jew nor Greek, Samaritan or Galilean ...

This clears things up and enables us to understand Jesus' admiration for the Samaritan. He sees in him a man whom the Holy Spirit has gripped, engendered, fashioned, led ... In the man's unstated prayer, Jesus hears the unspeakable groaning of the Holy Spirit. The Samaritan's whole course of action, his faith, his returning to Jesus, his prostration, the opening of his heart, his thanksgiving, his thirst for inner purity . . . all this to Jesus is the sign of the Holy Spirit in him . . . Christ, pure in heart and insight, sees in this man the presence of the Holy Spirit!

We must never forget, reader friend, that our thirst for purification, our thirst for cleansing, our efforts in pursuit of it, all are unceasingly animated, carried along, led by the Holy Spirit at work within us. How thankful we should be for this!

What wonderment this passage brings us as well; we see a Samaritan, the Holy Spirit within him, bowed down before the Son, giving glory to the Father . . . The Father, the Son, the Holy Spirit; this man, thus immersed in the presence of the Trinity is now mysteriously cleansed! "Stand up," Jesus says to him, "go your way; your faith has saved you!"

Each to his own way

Jesus' love for the Samaritan is so pure that it is void of any desire to have a hold over him, to in some way secure him. "Go your way," Jesus tells him, leaving him entirely free . . . Yet there he was, right in front of Jesus, a man who would have made an excellent disciple! No, Jesus doesn't say to him, "Come and follow me," but, "Go! Go your own way . . . !"

When he speaks likes this, Jesus is not simply sending the man away; he isn't, so to speak, handing him over to himself, nor to some unclean spirit which might grab a hold of him anew . . . with seven other spirits still worse . . . Jesus knows that the man has the Holy Spirit within him. He sees in him a disciple of the Holy Spirit, and leaves him to the Spirit without the slightest fear, in full confidence.

The account finishes with a separation; the Samaritan heads off in one direction and Jesus in another, leaving us with a curious impression. What was really going on?

Jesus chose to act in this way since not everything necessary for the man's well-being was yet accomplished. "Go your way," Jesus tells him, knowing that he himself had another road to travel. What road was this — where was Jesus heading?

Luke constructs his account in a wonderful way, giving us right at the outset the information which illuminates everything so very clearly: "Going up to Jerusalem . . ." Jesus was on the way to hand himself over in Jerusalem. The encounter with the Samaritan didn't alter his trajectory at all. He was following his own course. Was it to the Temple he was going? No, it was to Golgotha, to offer the sacrifice the Samaritan would no longer have to make for his cleansing, the sacrifice which is no longer necessary for you and I to make for our cleansing.

Jesus did not send the Samaritan to the priests, but would himself accomplish the sacrifice prescribed by the Law. What the man himself could not do to purify his heart, that which God alone could do, Jesus was to accomplish on the cross. Jesus, both priest and victim, frees us from sacrifices and every ritual of cleansing. By his own death, Jesus frees us and cleanses us to the deepest depths of our beings.

Jesus says nothing of this to the Samaritan; he does not explain what he will do in Jerusalem. Lowly of heart, he says nothing that would push himself forward. For him, it is enough just to say, in his great humility, "Stand up, go your way; your faith has saved you!"

"Stand up" in Greek is *"anastas,"* which also means "rise again"!

Rise again, friend Samaritan! Indeed, rise again, because Jesus is going to Jerusalem to die for you on a cross, outside the city, outside the camp, outside the sanctuary, as an exile, as unclean! Rise again, you, the leper, you who were dead to others and to God, with your torn garments, your banishment from prayer. Rise again; in his death you are now risen again!

Luke's account finishes here but without really being concluded; the most essential element is still to come! The text is left open, in suspense . . . opening onto a silence which invites us to ponder:

> One man, inhabited by the Spirit, ready to go his way giving glory to the Father . . .

> Another, also inhabited by the Spirit, pursuing his way to accomplish the will of the Father . . .

> The two of them united by the same Spirit, before the Father . . .

Lord Jesus Christ, Son of God,
Here am I, bowed down before you,
Full of the joy of knowing your presence.
Like the Samaritan, I give you my thanks:
You have opened a way where before there
    was none.
I give you thanks for the light you have shone in
    my heart,
The light of the purity received
In the new birth of the Holy Spirit,

The purity received with your gaze fixed upon me,
The purity received from the Father, mysteriously,
    in his grace.

Lord Jesus Christ, Son of God,
Like the Samaritan, here am I, bowed down
    before you,
I who also am profoundly unclean,
Here before you to plead:
Have mercy on me, come to my rescue,
I who leave open the door to unclean thoughts,
And allow them to enter and then defile.
Come to the help of my unclean prayer and make
    it clean.
Come to the help of my unclean love and make
    it clean.
Come to the help of my unclean mind and bring
    it light.
To you I pray, to you who alone are able,
To you who alone have offered sacrifice for us
To make us pure,
Pure with that final purity for which I still thirst,
But of which, at times, you give me a taste.
Be blessed, you, our Lord and our God,
With the Father and the Holy Spirit,
For ever and ever. Amen.

Chapter 2

ASKING FOR CLEANSING

WHAT ARE WE TO DO TO CLEANSE OUR HEARTS OF THE defilements left by impure thoughts? And what are we to do before that to prevent these thoughts from gaining a foothold within us? The first thing, say the Fathers, is to stand watch at the door of the heart, note carefully what thoughts present themselves and repel those that are impure. "Keep your heart," says the book of Proverbs (4:23). This indeed is where everything begins. Anyone who repels the impure thought before it becomes resident in the heart is not defiled by it, and the heart stays clean.

Repelling an impure thought very quickly takes on an aspect of combat since the thoughts are insistent and profit from any negligence as they seek to insinuate themselves into the heart; they seek to impose themselves on us, at times disguising themselves as thoughts of light! This is spiritual combat, an immense labor which mobilizes all our energies and indeed is too much for them; the task is far beyond our own strength. Our situation is the same as David confronted by Goliath. If we wish to emerge victorious from the fight, we have necessarily to count on God; to rely on his help; to follow his counsel; to do nothing without him. "Without me you can do nothing," Jesus says so truly. To experience the struggle in this way means, from start to finish, living by prayer.

However, it may be that, through negligence, our vigilance fails and our struggle founders on the rocks, leaving us beaten down, without protection against the impurity in our heart because of some victorious impure thought. This is not the moment to lower our arms in despair. On the contrary! This is the moment to do as did the leper, to bow down before the Lord, addressing this prayer to him: "Lord, if you are willing, you can make me clean" (Luke 5:12).

Psalm 51

Further to the simple and beautiful prayer of the leper, which we can appropriate for ourselves, we have in the book of Psalms another request for cleansing; there is just the one, but it is so beautiful as to be quite sufficient, and we can make it our own any time this becomes necessary. It is such an extraordinary prayer that, as John Cassian tells us, some of the monks of the Egyptian desert would repeat it every day. One of them, Abba Lucius, recited it continually, conscious as he was of the multitude of obstacles in his spiritual struggles.

This unique request for cleansing in Psalms is in Psalm 51. The psalm is well known, but it is generally considered a plea for forgiveness, though this is not altogether the case. In fact, the word "forgiveness" is absent, as is the verbal form "forgive." In contrast, in this psalm David does ask God to cleanse him, employing all the vocabulary of purification and the images that go in that direction; this invites us to consider the psalm as really a request for cleansing. In order to think closely about it, I propose to read the psalm from this angle.

To the chief musician, a psalm of David
When the prophet Nathan came to him,
After David had been with Bathsheba.

1. *Have mercy on me, O God, in your kindness.*
   In your great tenderness, wash out
   my transgressions.
2. *Wash me completely from my sin*
   And cleanse me from my fault.
3. *For I know my transgressions*
   And my fault is constantly before me.
4. *Against you and you only have I sinned*
   And done what is evil in your eyes,
   That you might be justified in your words,
   Beyond reproach in your judgment.
5. *Behold, I was born a sinner,*
   And in sin my mother conceived me.
6. *You desire truth deep within.*
   You will make me know wisdom in secret.
7. *Cleanse me with hyssop and I shall be clean.*
   Wash me and I shall be white as snow.
8. *Cause me to hear joy and gladness,*
   And the bones which you have broken shall rejoice.
9. *Hide your face from my faults,*
   Blot out my sins.
10. *Create in me a clean heart, O God!*
    And renew in me a well-disposed spirit.
11. *Do not cast me far from your presence.*
    Don't withdraw from me your Holy Spirit.

12. *Restore to me the joy of your salvation*
    And a vigorous spirit to sustain me.

13. *I will teach transgressors your ways,*
    And sinners will turn back to you.

14. *O God! God of my salvation!*
    Deliver me from blood,
    And my tongue will celebrate your righteousness.

15. *O my Lord, open my lips*
    And my mouth will publish your praise.

16. *Indeed, you have no pleasure in sacrifices.*
    That I should make a burnt-offering is not
    your desire.

17. *The sacrifices of God are a broken spirit;*
    A broken and a contrite heart,
    O God, you do not despise.

18. *In your kindness, do good to Sion,*
    Build up the walls of Jerusalem.

19. *Then you will be pleased with righteous sacrifices,*
    With burnt offerings and whole burnt offerings.
    Then bulls will be offered on your altar.[1]

Every day, John Cassian tells us, a monk would recite this psalm, thereby asking God for the cleansing of his heart since everyday he was assailed by impure thoughts which would so often got the better of him, leaving more or less deep defilements in his heart.

The psalm is so important that one of its verses is the first phrase spoken by monks of the Benedictine tradition

1. The translation here closely follows the French, with the exception of the verse numbering, which follows the normal English pattern. (Trans.)

each night before dawn: "Lord, open my lips, and my mouth will publish your praise" (v 15). With this verse the whole psalm is implicitly being prayed. When monks begin each day in this way it is because they know that the night so often allows into the heart a troop of impure thoughts; it therefore becomes indispensable to invoke God since he alone is able, in his grace, to cleanse the heart and dispose it towards praise.

Forgiveness and cleansing

Forgiveness and cleansing are such closely allied ideas that this psalm has come to be considered a plea for forgiveness when really it is more a quest for cleansing; this is not a serious problem since the two things together form part of the same complex. However, if we want to see more clearly into the idea of cleansing, it will be helpful to look at what distinguishes it from forgiveness; this will do away with any confusion. The two differ as a fault and an impurity differ, close though they are.

To forgive is to lift off, take away, a fault; while to cleanse is to take away the marks the fault leaves behind. There is a similarity with the way water works on iron, eventually producing rust. If we compare water to the fault, then taking the water away is like forgiveness. When the water is removed, the fault is forgiven, but the rust remains, and, for it to disappear, a second operation is required to return the iron to its former purity; this is purification, cleansing.

Impurity, however, is not always related to faults. Thus, to touch a dead body was not in the Old Testament considered a sin, but it was an act which made you unclean. A person who touched a corpse did not need to be forgiven but cleansed. The rules to be followed, stated in the Old

Testament on this subject, are indeed rituals for cleansing, not expiation.

The woman with the haemorrhage who wished to touch Jesus was not seeking forgiveness for her faults but healing and cleansing from the defilement involved in her continual loss of blood (Matt 9:20–22). In fact, while blood was seen as defiling, it did not make a person a sinner.

To have an unclean thought in the spirit does not necessarily mean that there is a sin. The issue that arises here is cleansing, not forgiveness.

I met a woman who was a prison visitor who told me how one day she had listened to a detainee recounting all the foul actions he had committed — and which delicately she chose not to tell me. When she left the prison she went home and had a long, long shower, feeling so dirtied internally by all she had heard. Her reaction is significant. She did not feel in any way guilty for the acts committed by the man, but she did feel defiled by his words. She had no need of pardon but instead of being washed, cleansed.

A dream that contains sins, even serious ones, is not sinful in and has no need of forgiveness. However, it can leave behind impure thoughts by which we feel soiled even when we wake, and sometimes long afterwards. Thoughts like these do not call for pardon but for cleansing of the heart.

These are examples which, it seems to me, help us appreciate the difference between forgiveness and cleansing.

Another difference appears in the feelings that stem from a fault as opposed to arising from an impurity. The feeling born of a fault is guilt; by contrast, the feeling born of impurity is one of unworthiness. The Samaritan leper, bowed down before Jesus, did not consider himself guilty but unworthy.

Conscious and unconscious sins

Sin we are aware of always defiles the one who commits it, so we then seek both forgiveness and cleansing. Is it the same though if the fault is unconscious; and does it leave behind the stain of impurity on the unconscious? If, for example, reader friend, I find out that by something I have said I have hurt you, quite involuntarily, I will ask your forgiveness but knowing at the same time that I have no feeling of impurity. The forgiveness I receive from you will have no need to be succeeded by cleansing. But will this unconscious fault in fact have left a mark on my unconscious?

This is a question to which I am not altogether sure how to respond, though it does seem to me that the unconscious fault is likely to leave some trace. Leading me to see things this way is the rite of baptism. In baptism we are in fact given both forgiveness and cleansing. The water of baptism washes and purifies inwardly, not only from known faults but those that are unknown; this is very clear in the case of the baptism of an infant.[2] The only sin of which an infant could be cleansed is the general sin diffused throughout humankind, commonly known as original sin. Sin of this nature is unconscious, as is the impurity allied to it but which is washed and cleansed in baptism. By baptism, God, then, purifies our unconscious from every impurity found there.

2. Clearly, DB's church tradition includes infant baptism. (Trans.)

In Psalm 51, David twice asks God to cleanse him of his faults (vv 2 and 7), and we see that the faults at issue are firstly conscious faults and then unconscious ones.

The title of the psalm draws our attention to faults committed consciously by David, his adultery with Bathsheba, and the other associated sin, the murder of Uriah, her husband. David had done everything possible to deliberately hide Uriah's murder. He had sent him into battle in the front line so that he would die fighting, and that is just what happened (2 Sam 11:14–21). In one sense, David himself had not killed him, his hands were clean! But his heart was not; he well knew himself to be responsible for the death and was therefore a murderer.

This was David's dealings with his conscious sins for which he sought cleansing (v. 2). After this request though, David went further in his prayer and spoke also of his unconscious faults, and cried out to God for cleansing from these too. This unconscious sin is specifically the sin which he had carried around from his birth, even from conception, and this really could not be a conscious fault (v 5). It was for this fault that David reiterated his request for cleansing in verse 9. The psalm is beautifully constructed: first there is the request for cleansing of known sins (v 2), then the uncovering of unknown faults (v 5), and finally he asks to be purified from these unknown sins.

How had David become aware of a fault so deeply buried in his unconscious? There is no doubt about this; it was the Holy Spirit helping him, the Holy Spirit who David knew to live in him, as seen in his request of God, "Do not withdraw your Holy Spirit from me" (v 11). Only the Holy Spirit can make clear to us the depths of our impurity, awakening us to what lies in our unconscious.

The question of delay

Another important difference between forgiveness and cleansing lies in the way forgiveness can be immediate, while cleansing may not be.

Forgiveness can be sought immediately after a fault is committed, and obtained without delay, up to seventy times seven times, according to Jesus! (Matt 18:22) When Jesus announced that the paralytic's sins were forgiven, the forgiveness took effect "immediately," Mark tells us (2:12). The sick man immediately took up his bed and walked, both healed and forgiven.

This immediacy of forgiveness can be felt by its beneficiary. It's a fact that if we go to someone to seek pardon and obtain it, the effect is felt straight away; we feel lighter, free, and this is often "immediately" after hearing the forgiveness expressed. It does not work the same way with cleansing.

A first delay

The Old Testament Law imposes a delay between defilement and the rite of cleansing. A person who touched a dead body, for example, could not be cleansed immediately but had to wait seven days (Num 19:14–16). I don't know just what this delay corresponds to, but it does need to be noted. In every case of defilement, the Law always imposed a delay between the time of defilement and the ritual of cleansing; the delay varied according to the defilement but there was a delay all the same; it was systematic. Thus the cleansing of leprosy extended over eight days, and these eight days were not compressible, even though in fact the prescribed rituals could all have been accomplished within a single day. This delay needs to be respected as a spiritual reality, the significance of which escapes me but needs to be observed; for myself, I hope that one day the issue becomes clear.

After the birth of a boy, the cleansing could not take place until the fortieth day (Lev 12:4), and for a girl not until the eightieth (Lev 12:5) . . . !

When it comes to internal defilements, there is a similar delay to be respected, as again we see in the case of leprosy, stretching across eight days, with the length of the eighth "day" being indeterminate, indicating the way the delay is in God's hands. Only God in his wisdom knows when a person who turns to him is really cleansed.

A second delay

Not only is there this first delay, but a second becomes evident in the biblical rituals for cleansing, not now between the defilement and the cleansing, but between the ritual and its efficacy. It is somewhat like taking aspirin; there is a delay between its ingestion and when its effects are felt.

Thus, when a person was purified from their contact with a corpse, the ritual for cleansing would be performed, but they remained unclean "until the evening" (Num 19:19), no matter the time of the ritual. The same is true of other purification rituals; the unclean person stayed unclean "until the evening" (Lev 11:25, 40; 15:5 . . .).

There is nothing similar with forgiveness; the moment it was pronounced, it took effect. From the moment we receive a word of forgiveness, we can feel its effect.

This is all so true spiritually. Although our guilt may disappear immediately following forgiveness, our sense of unworthiness tied to any impurity needs time to dissipate. Time is needed for the cleansing to become effective in the depths of the heart. What is the issue here? Is God unable to work more quickly? No! It has to do with our human nature, too opaque to rapidly assimilate the cleansing given.

When David says to God, "Purify me with hyssop and I shall be clean" (v 7), we can see how this request implicitly contains the two delays we have discussed. It does not mean, "Purify me now and I will immediately be pure," but rather, "Purify me when the first delay has run its course, and I will be pure when the second is concluded."

The delay in the perception of inward cleansing explains why we do not always immediately feel the forgiveness granted us. I remarked earlier that forgiveness can be felt immediately, but this is not always so. At times indeed we feel nothing of the forgiveness. Why? Is the forgiveness not real? Is it only partial, or in word only? No, the forgiveness is real, but, if we don't perceive it, it's because the fault forgiven has left within us its marks of impurity, and we need to wait to perceive the cleansing if we are to feel the forgiveness.

This is very important when we are dealing with the faults that God pardons. We can know ourselves to be forgiven by God without necessarily feeling the reality of it. In faith, we know we are forgiven, but we don't feel it. The forgiveness is real, effective and without delay, but it can't be felt until the delay tied to the accompanying cleansing has passed. The delay is variable in its length according to the faults, and often it is prolonged by further faults committed in the meantime. Therefore, do not despair, reader friend, if you have difficulty perceiving God's forgiveness; the forgiveness is real, but it is the inner cleansing which takes time.

The defilement of pride

When the heart is defiled by prideful thoughts, the mind is unable to enter into an understanding of the mystery of

God; we saw this with the disciples, prevented as they were by their proud thinking from entering into the mystery of the cross. Jesus had cleansed them by his word, as he told them when he washed their feet ("you are clean," John 13:10); but this didn't prevent their minds continuing in darkness because of the necessary delay while the cleansing took effect. It was not until after the cross and with the help of the Holy Spirit that the disciples were finally able to enter the mystery of the death of the Lord. Then their fully purified hearts began to burn, as two of them felt on the road to Emmaus (Luke 24:32).

The defilement of pride is more deeply engrained than any other mental defilement since it goes back to the beginning of time, to the serpent's bite, to the dawn of humanity, as we learn in the Genesis account. The cleansing antidote was given humanity on the cross, but the defiled human heart will remain impure "until the evening," that is, until the evening of mankind. When the evening finally comes, the cleansing effect of the cross will be felt by all. Then the promise of Jesus will accomplished perfectly and for all: "Blessed are the pure in heart, for they shall see God."

What are we to do as we await this evening, during the delay that separates the act of cleansing from the consciousness of its efficacy? We fight against every impure thought that can compromise the process by a new defilement; we pray, seeking God's help in the struggle; we pray asking him to shorten the delay; we pray, shedding tears, as Arsenius[3] wept until the evening of his life; and give thanks for the partial cleansings obtained in faith.

3. An early desert Father (350–445), much given to tears of repentance. (Trans.)

David's impasse

The first thing required of a sinner is to turn back to God in repentance by the confession of sins. David knew this well and speaks of his turning back in his prayer. Curiously though, he speaks of it in connection with others and not for himself: "I will teach transgressors your ways, and sinners will turn back to you" (v. 13).

Why does David not envisage this turning back for himself? Because it is not possible for him to turn back! His condition as a sinner impels him to turn, but his impurity prevents it! How can this be? It is a fact: the Law formally forbade an unclean person from entering the Temple (Num 19:13, 20) and so from any process of return to God!

We therefore see David in a total impasse, ready to turn to God and confess his fault, but prevented from doing so by his impurity. He describes his highly uncomfortable situation with a very strong image, saying to God that he has "broken bones" (v 8). David was nailed fast in place, unable to take a single step: his bones were broken! He even states that his bones were broken by God himself, which seems to show that God wished at all costs to prevent his approach, no doubt because his impurity was too great!

With this great blockage separating David from God, Satan could only exult! What was David to do? Pray? But prayer from an impure heart is impure itself and cannot reach God.

However, David prays just the same! His psalm is one hundred per cent prayer from start to finish. David dares turn to God in prayer; what audacity! Taking the thing to its logical limit, this might be seen as blasphemy. So what is the nature of Psalm 51, the audacity of faith, or indeed an almost blasphemous act of defiance aimed at God?

There is nothing in the psalm that looks like bravado; not a word of the prayer has the slightest hint of blasphemy; on the contrary! David's audacity has nothing of defiance in it; it all simply flows from the Holy Spirit. David knows it well; he knows the Holy Spirit lives in him, and it is the Spirit who impels him to prayer, who causes him to dare plead that he may be delivered from his impasse. This is why he cries out, "Do not withdraw your Holy Spirit from me!"

But then, if the Holy Spirit is in David, this would mean that God, by the Holy Spirit, has drawn near to him! This is extraordinary; David is unable to approach God because he is unclean, but God has come to him, despite his impurity! What grace, what love on God's part! He has come to seek David at the heart of his trouble, to deliver him from it. This, it seems to me, is the miracle contained in the psalm . . . How is this miracle to be described? Forgive me, reader friend, if I have difficult unwrapping this . . .

The more impure we are, the greater the impossibility of approaching God and the more impossible it is to pray. Also, though, the more I discover my impurity, the more this is a sign that the Holy Spirit is in me to uncover how impure I am. This comes to saying that before ever we seek to approach God for cleansing, God has approached us by his Spirit, not only to reveal our impurity, but also with the intent to cleanse; just his presence within is enough to cleanse, the presence of the one who is Pure who purifies.

The closer God comes, the more we discover our impurity; but also, the closer he comes, the more he cleanses!

I, the unclean, am too unworthy to pray; but he, the Pure, comes so close as to be in me by his Holy Spirit, who brings prayer to birth. Thus the prayer of an unclean man is made clean by the Holy Spirit. The first word of prayer is in itself a sign of its being purified and answered, that the heart is on the way to cleansing, thanks to the Holy Spirit who is there within.

I am unable to take one step forward because my bones are broken, but he makes himself so close that my broken bones begin to dance . . . ! Like the leper, I bow down, petitioning God to purify me, and giving thanks to him that he is already doing so . . .

The prodigal son

The parable of the prodigal son says all this very wonderfully. Having "come to himself" (Luke 15:17), what did the son discover deep within? Answer — the extent of his sin against his father. There was nothing he could do but return in search of pardon, but his impurity held him back, and the impurity was certainly very great since he had defiled himself with prostitutes and wound up among the most unclean of any animal, with the pigs! The son was aware of being absolutely unworthy of returning to his father's house, and indeed unworthy to be called his father's son (v 17). He needed to quit the pigs and the prostitutes, but even then he would carry the shame in his heart, just as the smell of pigs and prostitutes clung to his body; and there was no way this would escape his father's notice. The closer he got, the more his sense of unworthiness would deter him, even to the point of not proceeding.

Nevertheless, the unworthiness did not prevent the unclean son from returning! Something stronger encouraged him to return to his father, something else he had discovered deep in his heart at the moment he came to himself. What he had discovered and could find nowhere other than at home with his father was his father's love.

The son, then, found in himself both his unworthiness as a son, which would stop him from returning to his father, and his father's love, which urged his return. The father's love was present in his heart and was working in him. Although unworthy to be a son, the prodigal never stopped saying "my father" (v 19), since the love of the father was greater and stronger than his unworthiness as a son. The father's love would not be defiled by the stench of the pigs. So, after he came to himself, the son got up and set off to his father; or rather, the father's love caused the son to arise, impelling him to return, drawing him . . .

Similarly, having come to himself, David discovered the Holy Spirit within himself, enabling him to sense the love of God drawing him. The Spirit prompts and God draws. He draws with cords of love (Hos 11:40) which nothing can defile, not even the grossest impurity; and so David makes his approach in prayer, as suggested to him by the Spirit. By his Spirit, God has come in search of David . . . The wonderful, humble Holy Spirit works in secret, and in silence nudges, prods, pushes us towards the infinite grace of God who draws us.

"Be merciful to me, O God," David says at the very beginning of his prayer. God had already been merciful in bringing to birth this pure prayer in an unclean heart that was being purified by this action of prayer itself.

The sin barrier

The wall which causes the impasse is sin, and David says this very clearly: his sin is constantly before him (v 5). The barrier erected between David and God was not put there by God but by sin, and this sin had come as a beautifully appareled seduction.

When David speaks of his fault, he does so in terms to which we should pay close attention: "My fault is constantly before — face to face with — me," he says. David uses the word for "face to face" (*neged*) which is used in Genesis to describe the woman God had given the man as his spouse (2:18). David speaks of his fault using a feminine word as if to say that the fault which had become "face to face" with him was simply Bathsheba, now become his spouse. This was certainly David's fault, this woman who now, as his spouse, was constantly before him, between God and himself. His fault prevented David from advancing towards God, from returning to him.

It is a fault, states David, which he "knows" (v 3), using precisely the verb "to know" which indicates the most intimate love between a man and a woman (cf. Gen 4:1). That is my fault, says David. It[4] is constantly there between you and me, a barrier which I cannot skirt, to which I am deeply attached since I love it intimately!

David is here stating a profound spiritual truth of which sooner or later we need to become aware: we love our faults, those at least to which we are tied in some form of dependence and therefore often find difficult to acknowledge. The alcoholic, for example, though suffering in his dependence, also loves his bottle!

The greatest obstacle between God and ourselves is not so much the faults as the love we have of our faults! An impure love, often intimate, and deeply lodged within us! Only the Holy Spirit coming into our hearts can bring

4. In French, the pronoun here is feminine because the word for 'fault' is feminine, and while DB is clearly using the pronoun to refer directly to the fault, it could also refer to Bathsheba (also feminine), which makes sense with the last phrase of the paragraph, 'I love it (or her) intimately!' (Trans.)

to light a love still more deeply embedded, more intimate, God's love for us. The Spirit alone can bring us into the perceived fact of loving God more than we love our faults.

The greatest obstacle between God and ourselves is impure love, love made unclean through love of money, of power, of glory, of sensual pleasure, and of so many other idols . . . Only the love of God can surpass and cleanse these impurities and enable us somehow to love him with all our heart, all our soul, all our strength . . .

The impossible sacrifice

"Who may ascend the hill of the Lord and enter into the holy place?" is the question asked in one psalm (24:3). The response is clear: "He who has clean hands and a pure heart" (24:4). David knows very well that his impurity prohibits him from access to the Temple. He will not be able to offer sacrifices, and the priests will be unable to perform the acts of purification linked to the sacrifices, as for example, the sprinkling with hyssop.

David knows all this, but this doesn't prevent him in his boldness from addressing God with an unprecedented request, "Cleanse me with hyssop" (v 7). This sprinkling using hyssop was always tied to a sacrifice, but it was never God who performed the sprinkling! No ritual foresaw any such intervention from God, and neither had anyone ever made such a request! If it were not for the Holy Spirit by whom David knew himself to be inspired, there would have been something blasphemous in this, but there was no blasphemy! It was indeed the Holy Spirit inspiring David in this prayer, and he was inspiring him to such an extent that David himself had no idea of the depth of his petition. With what sacrifice is hyssop in fact connected?

If David, because of his impurity, could not approach the Temple and offer a sacrifice, what would be the sacrifice used by God in which to dip the hyssop? "Purify me with hyssop!" David asks nonetheless! If David was unable to offer a sacrifice, who would offer one? We might go to the extreme of supposing David might offer himself, spiritually, as a sacrifice, but even that is excluded because, for a victim to be offered in sacrifice, its bones must not have been broken (see Exod 12:46). But, David's bones were indeed broken . . .

David has no idea what sacrifice might be used by God, but all the same he asks for the cleansing sprinkling. God would know exactly where to dip the hyssop. David says nothing more on this subject, but his request does leave God the possibility of offering himself a sacrifice . . .

For us as Christians, David's request takes on an extraordinary depth, which the Epistle to the Hebrews illuminates: the sacrifice to be offered is the sacrifice of Christ on the cross (9:18–22). The blood the hyssop will be dipped in to purify the impure is Christ's. Only the Holy Spirit could have led David to address such a request to God: "Cleanse me with hyssop!"

Internal washing powder

Barred from going up to the Temple, David could nonetheless have stayed at home and observed certain rites of cleansing. In particular, he could have washed himself and his garments, but he seems not to have done any of that. There is no suggestion in the psalm of him performing any ritual. No doubt he was conscious of his impurity as being so deep that no simple washing could suffice, no more than would soap powder. How, indeed could he wash his heart? His hands had not touched Uriah's dead body; it was in the heart that the murder left the deepest defilement. To wash his hands would be completely futile, not to say hypocritical! The proverb says it well; no man can cleanse his own heart (Prov 20:9).

Constrained to do nothing, David makes still another proof of extraordinary audacity, and asks of God himself the impossible, "Wash me!" (vv 2 and 7).

Our word "wash" is not very clear because it relates both to the personal toilette and to the use of a washing agent. In Hebrew, by contrast, no confusion is possible; there is one verb "to wash" for the personal use and another for the use of an agent. David here uses the word "wash me" in the sense of "scrub me with a cleansing agent"! It is not "scrub my clothes," but "scrub me, bleach me!" David compares himself to a dirty garment, soiled by adultery and the blood of a murder. David's impurity of heart is like that of dirty clothing.

Neither David nor anyone else can scrub clean their own heart. There is no ritual in view for such a cleansing! Where is one to turn when the Law makes no provision? David's great boldness is that it is to God himself, once again, that he turns. The whiteness required is not whiteness of the skin (the skin of an oriental could never be whiter than snow!), but of the heart, compared here to cloth to which a cleansing agent will restore its original dazzling white, "whiter than snow" (v 7).

Is God able to intervene like this deep in the heart, where no one else can? David is so persuaded. His boldness is well founded and is confirmed later by the greatest prophets.

For many years at the outset of his ministry, Jeremiah stood against the people to denounce all their faults. Israel, considered to be the very spouse of God, was treated forthrightly as prostituted (Jer 3). Jeremiah did not mince his words! Then, a few years later, the same prophet adopts a new tone and calls out to the same people in quite different terms: "Virgin Israel" (31:4 . . .) he says, not to deplore her lost virginity but to affirm what the people were now, once again, in God's eyes.

God alone is able to transform a prostitute into a virgin, to give back the heart of a virgin to a prostitute! Only God's love is capable of such a miracle, by pure grace. The first word David pronounces in his psalm clearly shows he knew who he was speaking to: "Be gracious to me, O God!"

The continuation of the first verse contains great theological truth. David does not put forward his own virtues, none of his past works, none of his heroic actions, not even his faith. No longer is there anything pure about David. Nothing can be presented to God, not even extenuating circumstances! The only reality on which David can lean is the reality of God: "Be gracious to me in your kindness; in your great tenderness, blot out my transgressions." David is full of nothing but faults and the defilement of his sins. Only God could intervene.

The name which is too pure

David prays! He dares to pray! But he does so very conscious of his impurity. This is most apparent in particular in the way that he never dares once to pronounce God's proper name. It is already such a miracle for him to be praying! It is a miracle he can experience, but he doesn't go too far. David is both bold and humble, wonderfully humble and bold!

The first way God is addressed in the psalm, and the most frequent, is the simplest title possible, the most common: "God." Not even "My God," which would invoke a connection God might choose to disavow. David therefore stays with the very simple, "O God" (vv 1, 10, 14 and 17).

Towards the end of the psalm he permits himself to go a bit further, "O God, God of my salvation" (v 14). With this expression, David advances his great hope; God is the only one who can save him.

In the following verse, David crosses a further little boundary — "My Lord" (v 15); this is a lot, but it is not God's proper name, the Tetragram. The word, "Lord," David pronounces here is a title of God and not his proper name. This proper name is too holy, in fact, too pure, for impure lips to defile by pronouncing it.

"My Lord": with this title, David sets forth God's royalty, before which his station is that of servant. It is the lowest of vassals who here addresses a prayer to his Lord. Such a servant might at any moment have his standing revoked by God.

The miracle of prayer

This psalm is a true miracle, as we have already said. Only the Holy Spirit could make David's impure prayer pure. The Spirit himself prays through David and impels him to such audacity, though in humility. The reason for restating this, reader friend, is to say that this miracle can be reproduced in whoever thirsts like David to pray, always in humility.

This psalm has its place in the Book of Psalms so that it can be offered as our prayer. We can make it our own, above all if, like David, we are conscious of being the least of God's servants. Whoever knows themselves to be impure in the depths of their being, from the day of their birth and even from conception, whoever knows that there is no ritual of cleansing they can accomplish, can always appropriate this psalm. The psalm is intended for such people. The Holy Spirit will come to renew in them the miracle of prayer.

The boldness of the psalm is the boldness of the Holy Spirit who does not wish to abandon any of God's servants, not even the most unworthy. Do not forget this, reader friend. Do not forget to impart this to the person you meet who considers him or herself the most unclean and unworthy. Remember the Samaritan, doubly unworthy because of his disease and his ethnic origin, but who dared bow down, face to the ground, at the feet of Jesus, and so declare his thirst for cleansing.

The depth of sin

David was a twofold sinner in both his adultery and his act of murder. His doubling up of sin made him particularly unclean, but he used this brief period of repentance to examine himself and discovered that sin was still more deeply engrained in his life than just these acts. He discovered it at the remotest point he could see in his personal history, realizing that there was a great deal more than the adultery and murder; David realized that he was a sinner from the first moment of his life: "Behold I was born in sin and in sin my mother conceived me" (v 5). After everything, and down to the last capillary and individual cell, he was a sinner.

There are gross misunderstandings with regard to verse 7. One long held view is that David was accusing his mother of having sinned in his conception. Today there is a tendency to think that David was seeking to shift the blame for his faults and transfer them to his mother . . . This all rests on a poor reading of the verse. David was not seeking to avoid the blame or accuse someone other than himself, not even Bathsheba — whom he had seduced. What he is stating in verse 7 is the gravity of his condition; sin was so deeply engrained within him that God would be obliged to perform for him a cleansing well out of the ordinary.

To underline how exceptional his case was, David describes his conception in excessive terms. He doesn't use the classical term for "to conceive" (*harah*), but another word (*yaham*) which is reserved for animals, showing indeed that he considered himself nothing but a beast before God, a bestial person!

What could God do faced with this reality? What could he do to correct something that predated even conception? David has the audacity on this occasion to ask of God something which, again, he alone could do: "Create in me a clean heart!" (v 10). To create is an act reserved only for God; he alone in the Old Testament is the subject of the verb. People make, but God alone creates, and he does it as from nothing. He would be able to create a pure heart, without having to use the tiniest unclean iota of David. A new creation, radically new, straight from the hands of God; this is what David in his audacity was asking!

Not only this, but David was even asking God to be his own mother in this new birth. In this plea he appeals to the tenderness of God (v 1), his "mercy" in Hebrew, a term which is tied to the womb, and is suggestive of motherliness. God will be able from his motherly womb to bring to birth a new David with a pure heart! The psalm is incredibly bold!

Contact with the unclean

We saw with the Samaritan leper that physical unclean-ness is transmitted by touch. Anyone who touches some-thing unclean becomes unclean, with the exception of God, who is alone in not being defiled by contact with the impure, just as the sun is not soiled when its rays strike a dung-heap. God is not defiled by contact with the unclean, but this does not prevent the Law forbidding anything unclean from entering the sanctuary. Things which pertain to God must not be defiled.

If physical defilement is transmitted by touch, what about inner defilement? It is not transmitted by touch; no one becomes unclean by touching something impure of heart!

Inner defilement is, however, transmitted, and this takes place through words. How we need to know this! Thus the fact of recounting some particularly foul sin defiles the person who hears it; this is the case in particular with sins of a sexual nature, so that telling such a matter awakens impure thoughts in the listener, which then defile them. A confessor needs to be attentive and guard against ques-tioning to obtain all the details; the further the questioning goes, the greater is the risk of their own heart being defiled.

Confessors have to learn to listen while protecting them-selves. How is this to be done? Well, in particular by tears. If in fact what is heard brings on tears, then these tears are a gift from God to cleanse. Therefore, let the tears flow! They purify and are able to cleanse even the person confessing the fault, as I was told by someone who, as confession was made, saw the confessor begin to weep. Seeing these tears, the person felt cleansed by them . . . Blessed tears!

Extreme discretion

In this psalm, David observes great discretion, not recounting a single detail of his failings. Were it not for the title, we would with difficulty suppose that this was the confession of an adulterer! "My fault is ever before me": this is the only detail which alludes to the adultery with Bathsheba! This truly is more than discreet! As for the murder, where is this mentioned? "Deliver me from the guilt of bloodshed!" (v 14). This, again, is very discreet!

Would David have been afraid of defiling God by his confession? Surely not, because this is impossible! Rather, he doubtless wished not to wound God more than he already had by his actions. Above all, though, David would not have wished to reawaken the unclean thoughts in himself. This too is a reality of which we should be aware; when we recount certain faults in detail, we revive the impure thoughts in our hearts connected to the deeds. To remind oneself, to run over a failing in detail, can often mean committing the sin again in one's heart. This is what David wishes to avoid, which is why he is so discreet. He is aware that God knows everything, and that is enough. What matters is the request for cleansing, not the revelation of impurity! David dwells not on his faults but on the plea for cleansing, which he formulates in so many ways, using different images: cleanse me with hyssop, blot out my faults, wash me . . .

With the image of the hyssop, David limits himself to a request that would have God intervene without the need for touch: sprinkling takes place at a distance. In the other images, by contrast, God's intervention implies direct contact, which is even bolder in the demand it makes on God.

Wash me and I shall be whiter....

The cleansing agent David to refers has nothing to do with our modern powders; according to the advertising it's enough to soak the offending article using the product — out it comes completely clean and we haven't so much as touched it! In David's time it was quite different; the agent was an abrasive which was vigorously applied to the clothing; the more abrasive the agent and the more it was trodden, trampled in, the cleaner the wash.

In all the rituals for cleansing, each person was to wash their own clothing, even the Levite (Num 8:21) and the priest (Num 19:7). Nobody was to have another person wash their garments for them! When another person was used to do the washing this was never for a ritual of cleansing; this would only be for a non-religious, profane occasion. This kind of washing had nothing to do with the sanctuary!

"Wash me — abrasively! — O God!" What nerve to involve God in an activity as profane as this! No one other than David had ever dared think of God as a washer-woman! David must have felt particularly dirty to have asked God such a thing! It was requiring God to be particularly humble if he was to do as asked!

O my Lord, open my lips!

The acts for which David is looking to God are very diverse: after asking for this particularly vigorous intervention, he goes on to a new request which this time supposes a touch of rare gentleness, no longer now with the feet, but with a hand, with the simple touch of a finger: "Open my lips!"

To open the lips of someone who is seeking this gesture, one would need to be full of great gentleness. This most beautiful image is however an extremely bold request since David's lips were as impure as the rest of his body. His whole body was unclean. In a worse condition than Isaiah, David was bound to cry out in the presence of God, "Woe is me! I am lost for I am a man of unclean lips!"(Isa 6:5).

In response to Isaiah's cry, a seraphim intervened on God's behalf and cleansed the prophet, while, however, maintaining a certain distance. He did not directly touch Isaiah's lips, having recourse instead to tongs and a burning coal. David, however, was not looking for any intermediary or instrument . . . he wished God to be involved directly through the touch of his hand on his lips!

What boldness, but equally, how lovely! The gesture David asks supposes great intimacy. "O my Lord!" he exclaims as he makes his request. In this title there is the great respect which is an element of the intimacy. David knows God sufficiently well to know that he will be humble, and close enough to touch the lips of a person who thinks of himself as the most unworthy of servants! What great intimacy! It would be enough for God to lay only a finger, in silence, on David's mouth to enable an overflow, not of the stream of impurity in his heart but of a flood of praise: "O my Lord, open my lips and my mouth will declare your praise!"

Saint Benedict called on each monk to leave the silence of the night behind by addressing this same request to God; this supposes the same boldness, the same intimacy, as well as the great modesty which dares to presume God's caress or the kiss of his lips . . . What a privilege to be able to leave the night behind in this way every new morning!

In the sanctuary of the heart

It is almost at the end of the psalm that David asks God to open his lips; this is to say that to this point they had been closed, so the prayer had not been spoken aloud. The psalm was spoken inwardly in the heart.

So David had not spoken out loud! No doubt he had not dared. No one, not even Nathan had been a witness to what God alone could hear. David would have been ashamed to expose to others all he had said, both its boldness and his uncleanness . . .

If, though, David had prayed with his mouth shut, in his heart, this also means that God, if he was to hear a prayer that was so inward, must himself have been present in David's heart. Indeed he was; anyone who prays internally knows that God is there in his or her heart.

By his presence alone God cleanses any place, wherever it might be, and transforms it into a holy place. We see that David had become a sanctuary! This is a final twist which may well cause us to marvel! David, so unclean, forbidden access to the Temple, and yet here, before he had spoken a single word, God had left the holy place and drawn near in silence; he took up residence in an unworthy heart he was now cleansing! What a marvel! The first word of the psalm sounded out in David's heart as in the Temple . . .

Exactly in what state, though, was David's heart? Towards the end of the psalm David speaks to just this point: "A broken and a contrite heart, O God, you will not despise" (v 17).

A brief change of direction

Just before he speaks of his broken heart, David stops using the second person to speak to God and uses the third person. He does this just the once, in one verse, in this particular phrase: "The sacrifices of God are a broken heart." Immediately afterwards he reverts to the second person through to the end of the prayer.

What is the meaning of this short and discreet disengagement, with its effect of holding God at a slight distance, brief moment though it is?

David has just been saying that sacrifices do not please God; he is therefore about to say what it is that does please God . . . but this is a rather difficult thing for him to say since it is the broken spirit or human heart!

A broken heart is a suffering heart! What kind of a God is this who takes pleasure in human suffering? A sadist? David is walking through a minefield!

He knows that he is approaching a very delicate issue, requiring great tact on his part, great reserve. The use of the third person indicates the extreme care which David wishes to observe with such a difficult matter.

It is obvious that God is no sadist. David is close enough and intimate enough with the Lord to know this and not to be suggesting anything so crude. What is it then that he is saying?

If God finds a certain pleasure in David's broken heart, it's because God's heart is also broken, wounded . . . and his wound is the result of David's sin. David knows he has wounded God and this is a subject it is difficult for him to discuss: "Against you and you alone have I sinned," he had said earlier (v 4), but without evoking the suffering he inflicted on God. He sensitively does not mention God's pain, but we surely hear it in his reserve.

David cannot find words to acknowledge God's pain. It is too difficult to speak of this, at the same moment, indeed, as God is suffering . . . So what David does talk about is God's pleasure! What pleasure? The pleasure of consolation brought by David's pathway of repentance, a process that does indeed console God.

It pains David to have hurt God. He opens up his wounded heart to God and this is the place from which he asks his forgiveness. The broken heart of a penitent consoles the person he offended.

God's pain because of the sin, and the consolation wrought by repentance — this is what David is trying to say here, with all the finesse of which he is capable:

Indeed, you have no pleasure in sacrifices.
That I should make a burnt-offering is not your desire!
The sacrifices of God are a broken spirit.
A broken and a contrite heart,
O God, you do not despise.

God is silent!

When a wounded heart is receiving comfort from the person who did the wounding, the comfort finds its best expression in silence . . .

David is then silent in turn!

Silence is joined to silence . . .

David knows he has been received, cleansed by the one who draws so very near . . .

Lord, my God,
Whose heart is broken, bruised by my behavior,
Come in silence to touch my lips
That praise may leap from my mouth.
My heart is broken,
But your act of tenderness will heal its wounds,
Your act of humility will pacify my pain.
I give you thanks,
You who welcome such as me,
To cleanse me with your love.
Let me enter now into silence,
Into your silence, in contemplation of you,
In that encounter my sin had fouled
But which your Holy Spirit makes possible,
Impelling me towards you,
To you who draw me with bonds of infinite tenderness.
Let thanks be rendered to you, eternally. Amen.

Chapter 3

CLEANSING TEARS

How does God effect our cleansing?

WE HAVE ALREADY SEEN THAT HIS PRESENCE ALONE WILL accomplish it; this is a wonderful miracle, a wonderful mystery! While our impurity forbids our approach to God and our inner leprosy keeps us at a distance from him, the Lord thinks it good, in his infinite grace, to draw near to us and to touch us by the outshining of his grace; he cleanses us, as the sun cleanses without being defiled in any way by the objects on which its rays alight. By his presence, then, God cleanses us, and this is enough! How wonderful!

God approaches in Jesus Christ, the only one who is pure and who is not defiled by contact with impurity, but who, on the contrary, purifies anything impure he touches. What more could we want? The story of the leper has shown us that when Jesus fixes his gaze on the unclean, he cleanses! Just by looking at us, Jesus makes us clean . . .

God also cleanses by his word as it makes its way into our hearts, as a ray of light chases away darkness.

God cleanses by the Holy Spirit; he too operates in our hearts, enabling us to hear the Word, bringing prayer to birth as he purifies every unclean thought in the secret place of a heart transformed into a holy temple.

The more we discover in ourselves the depths of our impurity, and the more we open ourselves to God, the closer God comes with his cleansing. Like the Samaritan leper, we bow down before the Lord in supplication and thanksgiving, pondering the miracle of the cleansing, without being able to fully grasp it.

Cleansing water

With regard to the great mystery of God's cleansing activity within us, I would like to dwell on one point, based on one concrete, material element God uses to cleanse.

In the Old Testament, there are three aids to cleansing, water, fire and blood. God uses these three elements as means which enable his purifying actions. He can cleanse without them (by his word, by his presence, by his Holy Spirit, as we have said), but also through them, since they enable us concretely to receive the cleansing. With the goal of teaching us, God uses whatever will help us better perceive his work within us.

Water, fire and blood; the three elements can relate to the three persons of the Trinity, the purifying fire relating to the Holy Spirit who burn away our impurities, the blood surely referring to the blood of Christ which cleanses us, and the water, which we can be set in relation to the Father, though in a way that is less obvious.

I don't intend here to go further into the effects of the fire and the blood; this is not because they are negligible but just because it is not possible for me to fit so much into this short book. Many works have been written about the cleansing blood of Christ, shed on the cross. This remains central, though it is not what we will examine here.

So, without overlooking the fire and the blood, I wish now to pause over the cleansing of water and think closely about it; this for me is also a way to focus a little more on the place of the Father in the work of cleansing. The account of the leper principally concerns Christ, the Son of God; Psalm 51 above all brings to light the cleansing work of the Holy Spirit in David's heart; what then is the role of the Father in our cleansing? This is what we will now examine closely.

Tears of repentance

God has at his disposal all the water he might wish for our cleansing, but there is one form of water in particular on which I would like to dwell as something offered to him in an amazing way. I am thinking of tears, and above all the tears shed by those who are seeking cleansing from God. Whether these tears are those that actually flow down our cheeks, or those that are shed inwardly in the heart, it matters little! It is always the case that "tears" go along with every movement of repentance, each petition for cleansing. They are always there when God is called on to cleanse.

The Fathers paid close attention to tears, and most particularly to tears of repentance, the sort of tears of which David, for example, speaks in one of the prayers in which he confesses sin: "Lord, do not punish me in your anger, and do not chastise me in your fury . . . I am eaten up with crying; each night my bed is bathed by my tears, my bed clothes are soaked as they fall . . ." (Ps 6:1, 7)

Like David, hidden away in the solitude of his bed chamber to weep, the Fathers took refuge in their cells, Abba Arsenius for example; they did so not simply out of a sense of reticence lest others see their tears, but to deeply and without ostentation experience the demands of repentance. Tears play such a large role in repentance that in the Fathers the expression "to weep over one's sins" becomes synonymous with "to repent." There is no repentance without tears.

The clearest gospel model of this is Peter, who began to weep after the crowing of the cock when he realized that he had denied Christ. The three synoptic gospels specify Peter's weeping at this moment and that he "went out" so that that his tears not be seen (Matt 26:75, Mark 14:72, Luke 22:62). He took refuge in the solitude of the night to shed his tears, with God alone as witness. Weeping over one's sins is done before God alone, in the deepest darkness.

The Fathers sought refuge in their monastic cells, in the dark of their hearts, and there, buried away in prayer, they were given to discover the secret of tears. Then the sorrowful tears of repentance were transformed into tears of joy, deep sadness into wonderful goodness. At the end of the tears, joy unspeakable is found . . .

To enable others to share their blessing, though never managing to fully convey something that is after all beyond expression, the Fathers invite us to true repentance. No endeavor to contrive these tears is necessary; we can have confidence in God, in the full hope that it will also be given to us in turn to discover the secret of tears, in the mystery of "joyful sadness" as one of the Fathers says.

From impurity to pure tears

We are capable of shedding all sorts of tears, tears of mourning, anger, remorse, of joy, well-being . . . but tears of repentance have something very particular about them. They are born of a fresh consciousness of sin and of the defilement of heart allied to this; they begin to flow because of the abundance of sins and are shed in God's sight as forgiveness is sought. They are impure tears, freighted with all the impurity of our hearts: "Each night my bed is bathed by my tears, my bed clothes are soaked as they fall . . ."

The mystery is that these tears so often contain in themselves a surprising and very real purity, even while they display before God the full extent of our impurity! It can seem amazing that an unclean person is able to shed pure tears! What a mystery! For myself I have had the privilege of seeing men of impure hearts draw near to God in repentance and shed before him tears of extreme purity . . . The deeper and truer the repentance, the purer the tears! How can this be? Didn't Jesus say that everything that issues from an unclean heart is unclean and defiles the man? But tears can indeed issue from the unclean inner man!

All that finds its source in impurity is impure, it's true — but with the exception, at times, of tears! Here we find a great mystery, one which brings us to silence as we come to contemplate tears such as these.

Jesus never said anything about tears! Did he wish to keep their mystery a secret? I believe so. "I have many other things to say to you," he declared to his disciples, "but you cannot bear them now" (John 16:12). Later, perhaps? When the Holy Spirit has come and leads us into all the truth . . .

An appeal to the Fathers

When Peter, with the discovery of his sin, weeps, Matthew and Luke specify that he wept "bitterly" (Matt 26:75, Luke 22:62). When a penitent reaches the point of weeping over his faults he discovers how bitter tears can be. But while there are these bitter tears, there also sweet tears: tears of joy are sweet indeed, and so are tears of happiness.

Despite speaking of bitter tears, the Bible never mentions the alternative, so when it came to speaking of these, the sweet tears, the Fathers had to rely solely on their own Holy Spirit illuminated experience, and it is they, reader friend, confronted as we are by this silence of the Bible , that I propose that we follow on this topic, always looking out for any occasion where the Bible might be able to light our way.

Among the Fathers, one excellent witness is John Climacus, who devotes an entire chapter of his celebrated "Ladder of Divine Ascent" to tears. Living in the Sinai desert during the seventh century, this monk had behind him a long spiritual tradition which he had assimilated perfectly; and then there was his own experience of more than forty years of the hermit's life, which had seen him draw alongside a host of penitents; in short, he knew what he was talking about when it came to tears!

As a good monk, solicitous of repentance and well versed in the Bible, he most surely knew about bitter tears, having shed them himself in his retirement. These tears of "compunction," the word for the sorrow due to consciousness of one's faults before God, are not only bitter, he says, but also "sorrowful" (7.50).[1]

More though, John Climacus also knew sweet tears and speaks of them with real enthusiasm. For him they are of such a particular nature that he came to think of them as having a different source to the others. Here is what he says: "As well in nature as in the matter of compunction, we need to distinguish between things which spring up spontaneously and those which have an external moving

1. The references in the following passage are those of the text of The Ladder of Divine Ascent used by DB. They vary in different translations. (Trans.)

source." He goes on to explain: "When our soul, without any deliberate effort on our part, melts into tears and we find ourselves softened and peaceful, then make haste (run)! The Lord has come and hasn't waited to be asked!" (7.28)

The hermit of the Sinai marveled with good cause; there are days when our tears start to flow on their own, with such sweetness that we are made entirely tender and peaceable. A phenomenon as marvelous as this could only have one explanation, that the tears are triggered by God and attest that he has visited us on his own initiative, when we have not sought it.

Climacus' statement is truly superb and witnesses to a spiritual life of great richness and depth. His perception seems perfectly just to me, as so many of the Fathers subsequent to him were able to confirm. When such sweet tears flow from our eyes, reader friend, we make haste, we "run" indeed, hurrying to bow down and adore the one who does us the grace to visit us. These tears are so beautiful that Climacus never fails to say that they are a "gift of God" (cf. 7.8, 14, 52, 54, 55 . . .), and how true this is! Here then is a first great fact to affirm, that there are tears which come from God.

Joyous sorrow

Pressing on further with his remarkable analysis, John Climacus observes most perceptively that these sweet tears often slip their way into the very heart of the bitter tears: "When I consider the nature of compunction I am amazed; how can what we call an affliction and sorrow contain in itself, hidden at its core, so much joy and lightness, as wax contains honey?" Our hermit made sure he answered his own question: "God consoles the broken heart in secret" (7.54).

This is altogether both just and wonderful; tears of sweetness, which is to say the tears that God gives us in the midst of our tears of repentance, are God's consolation in response to our tears as we seek pardon. How wonderful it is of God to pardon us at the very heart of our plea for pardon, and then to manifest his pardon by a sign that is both concrete and very discreet. This discretion reveals the way in which God hides himself in his humility, the humility of love acting with a finesse replete with gentleness. The gentle sweetness of these tears flows from the gentleness of God, from his infinite tenderness. It is so wonderful . . .!

As he remarks how bitter tears can suddenly contain such sweetness, and how the astringency of repentance opens onto the sweetness of forgiveness and consolation, John Climacus provides an excellent response to an essential question we all have as to how the penitent can know he or she is forgiven. By what sign can it be recognized? Climacus' response seems spiritually so accurate to me. I know that I am forgiven when my bitter tears turn sweet. How, indeed, could tears be transformed from bitterness into sweetness? This is not within our power! It is something God alone can do! Not only that, but again, as our hermit finely comments, God does it in secret, in a hidden way. He was right, and there is no other explanation but that our humble God steps in, in such a discreet way, at the very source of our tears . . . We praise and bless him for such humility and such attentive consideration for the penitents that we are!

"God in a secret way consoles the broken heart": this fine phrase of Climacus is an integral follow-up to the phrase in Psalm 51: not only does God "not despise a broken and contrite heart" (Ps 51:19) — he consoles it!

John Climacus continues with the same discernment, and I receive what he says as truly inspired. The gentle tears, he says, are "pure tears that cleanse" (7.37), not indeed because of their own efficacy but because they are a means used by God to cleanse. "As fire consumes stubble, so tears wash out all the impurities, both open and hidden." (7.35) This is very fine; through these gentle tears, God cleanses the impurities from our conscience; this in itself is a great matter, but he also cleanses the impurities from our unconscious, which is more beautiful still. How marvelous and what a release! What a gift of God — that he should purify our unconscious of all its defilements!

Thus are bitter tears transformed into sweet tears. John Climacus' wonderment is expressed in a paradoxical formula whose secret was well known to the Fathers, that in the tears we find the "joyous sorrow" of both compunction and consolation (7.11). What wonderful good news, that at the very heart of repentance, God gives his pardon and cleansing; a joyous sorrow, indeed! It is not possible to hope for a greater benefit from God than this.

"Joyous sorrow"; this paradoxical formulation explains the title given by the hermit of Sinai to the seventh step of his Divine Ladder, "Of the affliction that produces joy."

In all that John Climacus says here, reader friend, I recognize our Lord, who at Marah performed a miracle for his people which casts a new light on tears. There at Marah, we are told, the Lord transformed the bitter waters into sweet (Exod 15:25). In the wilderness of our lives and the aridity of our repentance, God performs again the same miracle on the springs of our soul; he transforms the bitter tears of repentance into sweet, signifying his cleansing comfort.

Did David weep as he spoke Psalm 51? This we are not told, but why should it not be so? Hadn't he stated in another psalm, "Every night my couch is bathed with my tears, my bed soaked by my crying" (6:7)? Whatever the case, John Climacus felt able to affirm to anyone who prays Psalm 51 that, "The tears of this most holy love make very clear to us that our prayer has been accepted" (7.9).

Baptismal water and tears

Many of John Climacus' statements show how fully this man of prayer was saturated with Psalm 51. To the references in what has been said so far, I will add this: "Tears *efface* the faults we commit" (7.8), which echoes David's petition, "According to your great mercy, *efface*, wash away, my transgressions" (51:3), "*blot out* my iniquities" (51:11). Climacus is very insistent, that the Lord "presents us with the sponge of sorrow (sorrow which is precious to him) and the refreshing water of tears that are agreeable to God, in order to soak up, blot out, expunge the record of our crimes" (7.28).

There is one point, however, on which Climacus differs from the psalm, which is that he doesn't think in terms of clothes being washed in water with detergent; his outlook is more personal. This change is explained very naturally by the importance he accords baptism, which he views as a bath in which we are washed. According to him, the connection between tears and baptism is so close that he even affirms with remarkable spiritual assurance that, "The waters of Jordan flow from the eyes in torrents of tears" (26.151). We understand that the water of baptism, the tears, all of it, is given by God to cleanse us of our faults. However, by making such a very close correspondence, Climacus raises tears to the level of sacrament. This is very bold on his part, but still doesn't go as far as what he proceeds to say next.

This holy man of God goes much further, indeed, with an audacity he was well aware of, and which, it seems to me, is in the same vein as David's numerous audacities in the Psalm; an inspired boldness!

This is what he says: "This fountain of tears after baptism is greater than the baptism itself, as audacious as this affirmation may be. Baptism, in fact, purifies us from the faults which preceded it, while the tears wash away the faults which we commit later. As baptism is received in infancy, we have all defiled it, but we renew it (in tears) to its original purity. If God, in his love for people, had not given us tears, how difficult and rare it would be to find those who are saved" (7.8).

What boldness indeed, to place tears above the sacrament of baptism! What impelled this holy man to such outspokenness? It is the certainty that the tears are given by God, that they come from his love, as he affirms — "if God in his love had not given tears." Everything provided by God in love is beyond price.

Climacus provides us rather finely with an answer to the Christian's sad question as to how, once baptism has been received and we have therefore been cleansed, we can be cleansed of faults committed subsequently. What water can be substituted for the water of baptism, given that baptism cannot be repeated? We are only baptized once. John Climacus' response is splendid, that the water of baptism only flows once, while God himself gives the tears that flow as often as there is repentance. This constant fact, granted by God himself, puts tears above baptism.

To my knowledge, Climacus' audacity did not send a shudder through any Church Father; not one of them disowned it. I can cite one, one of the most notable, Gregory the New Theologian, who has for me the merit of anchoring his view in the Gospel, in the words of Jesus: "Spontaneous tears spring up painlessly; they cleanse the penitent and confer a second baptism on him, the baptism the Lord spoke of in the Gospel, that "unless a man is born of water and the Spirit he cannot enter the Kingdom of heaven" (John 3.5). Gregory is also very bold, daring to speak of a "second baptism" and then to define it as a baptism of tears!

Discernment

John Climacus is nevertheless prudent about tears, knowing very well that not all are given by God. We have to know how to discern. "Do not trust your tears before your soul is perfectly cleansed" (7.39).

In fact, "tears are born of multiple, diverse causes . . . of nature, of God, of some harmful tribulation or of something praiseworthy, of vainglory, of lust, of charity, of thoughts of death or many other possible sources" (7.36)

It is simply a fact that no one could say that all tears come from God.

We must not confound emotions with spirituality. Not every tear is a gift of God. In summary, we could say that there are three types of tears, natural tears (from pain, from strong feelings . . .), wrong tears (in relation to the passions), and spiritual tears, given by God (7.38).

Continuing to look at spiritual tears, tears given by God, there is one point in reading John Climacus which remains obscure in that he doesn't really speak about the source of the tears. They come from God to be sure, but isn't there more? Can't we be more precise?

The hermit of Sinai goes no further since he thought of himself as already having been very bold. There is a certain reserve in his writings which we need to respect, but one small phrase we have already cited causes me to think that he knew a little more, that he dared not discuss.

Here is the phrase which holds my attention: "The tears from the Most Holy Love demonstrate to us that our prayer has been accepted." Should "most holy love" be written with capitals or not? Does the expression point to the love of God or ours? Are the "tears of the Most Holy Love" shed by us or indeed by . . . God?

Boldness hidden by silence

When we talk about our tears, is our love great enough to be described as "most holy"? I doubt it! No one is "most holy" except God himself! Climacus leaves us in uncertainty, never quite allowing himself to say that God might shed tears! No doubt this was a venture too far, touching too far into God's intimate concerns. Climacus thinks he has been quite bold enough already!

Nevertheless, if there are tears which are above and beyond the sacrament of baptism, how could they be simply human? How would we not turn our thoughts to God's tears as being more able than baptismal water to feed the fountain of our own tears? Why wouldn't we consider the purity of God's tears if we want to find the source of any purity in our own tears? Might not God, in giving us the gift of tears, give us his very own tears? It does make things clear; our pure tears, which so cleanse us, would in fact be the very tears of God mingled with our own.

Was this what Climacus thought? It does seem to me that this is so, but he preferred to keep it to himself in the secret of his hermitage, in the secrecy of his intimacy with God . . . How blessed you were, holy hermit!

If he dared not speak openly about God's tears, it would be because the theological context of his period did not permit it, certainly in the Greek milieu to which he belonged; the tears of God, in fact, were unimaginable because the dominant Greek philosophy said that tears were a sign of imperfection. God is perfect; he doesn't cry! It seems to me that, like John Climacus, the Greek and Latin Fathers who did think that God could cry, also dared not say so!

In tune with the Hebrew

What makes me bold about this in our day is not simply the evolution of theology, or our general mentality, but the Bible itself. How so? Surely John Climacus knew the Bible, and perhaps rather better than me.

Reader friend, there is something we need to know; the Bible used by the Fathers is not altogether the same as ours, in particular, the Old Testament. Let me explain. The Old Testament we read today is from the Old Testament Hebrew and our translations have that as their starting point; however, the Greek Fathers, which is to say, those who most strongly marked Christian theology, all used the Greek Old Testament, the Septuagint. Now, when it comes to the tears of God, the Septuagint never speaks of them, absolutely never! By contrast, the Hebrew Old Testament does, very discreetly, but they are mentioned. Climacus and the other Greek Fathers, not reading the Hebrew, were never able to read what the Bible says about God's tears, and it is certainly this which held them back from speaking on the subject. What a shame! What wonderful commentaries they would have written had they known! But there we are . . .

For their part, the Latin Fathers, using a Bible translated from the Hebrew, might have had an understanding of God's tears. Nonetheless, they followed in the footsteps of the Greek Fathers; the influence of Greek thought was very strong!

We are therefore going to move on from the Fathers and turn to the Hebrew Bible, to find what is said there about God's tears, this time with the rabbis for company.

The tears of God in Jeremiah

The only book in the Bible which puts God and tears together is Jeremiah. Perhaps this is not by chance; God no doubt chose the one man most inclined to tears to speak to him of his own. Unfortunately, Christian commentators have a tendency not to make a distinction between the prophet's tears and God's.

The most explicit passage about the tears God sheds is found in the mouth of God himself: he turns to his prophet and charges him with a message, the tenor of which, concerning his intentions towards his people, is without parallel: "Speak to them this oracle: that my eyes run down with tears night and day without ceasing, because the virgin, my people, has been struck a grievous blow" (14:17).

This is the nature of God's altogether surprising confession to his prophet, who we might think of more as his intimate, given the way God shares with him things he had not said, not even to Moses or Abraham, or any other of his friends. Jeremiah here becomes, in a way, God's confidant: "Speak to them these words — that my eyes run down with tears night and day without ceasing, because the virgin, my people, has been struck a grievous blow . . ." And that's it; God adds nothing more, but it is a very great deal!

The first attitude to adopt before a divine confession like this is silence. What are we to say? The angels and archangels are silent! What God has said can only be received in silence, the heart overwhelmed . . .

"Speak to them these words . . ." Did Jeremiah ever pass on what God had told him? We don't know. Certainly, it is not recorded that he spoke to the people about God's tears, or that he made any comment on them. He was perhaps content just to dictate the divine confession to his secretary, Baruch, who conscientiously committed it to writing, and leave it there. It is ours to read this passage and to allow ourselves to be exercised by it in the deepest, most secret place of the heart.

Reader friend, I would like not to have anything further to say . . . !

If I now continue, it is only after numerous days of silence . . .

This confession of God's is so extraordinary that still today there are commentators who think that the tears are Jeremiah's and not God's; that God was calling on his prophet to tell the people that he, Jeremiah, was weeping: "Tell them that you weep!" This is an interpretation which shows the degree to which Christian tradition, a stranger to the idea that God might weep, continues to mark the way we read the Bible. Once we disengage from the traditional influence, it becomes possible for us to hear what this text is in fact saying, even if it is difficult to do so; it is not, "Tell them that you weep" but rather, "Tell them that I weep."

Jeremiah did not witness God's tears; all he did was hear God speak of them, without him showing them. No one has been a witness to God's tears. How could one do so and retain life? It would be unbearable; indeed no one can even see God and live! His glory alone is too great for our feeble eyes; and if, still more, we were to have before our eyes the glory of God in tears, and more yet, tears on our behalf, we would be so overwhelmed as to die of it!

Indeed, the cause of God's tears is us, his people; "the virgin, my people," as God says, with the depths of love the word "virgin" carries in the mouth of God. The tears of God are of an unfathomable depth of love and compassion.

The message which Jeremiah was called upon to transmit was to be a wonderful comfort to the people. There is in fact nothing more beautiful. Faced with the compassionate tears of God, the people could not but experience profound peace and themselves shed tears of great sweetness, the pure tears of a virgin discovering the extent to which she is loved by her Lord, purified by the compassion of her God.

The verse preceding God's confession shows that it is much more than tears of compassion; the tears are tears of grief. In fact, the virgin has been "dealt a terrible blow" and is so wounded she is bound over to death, to abandonment in the street, without burial! God announces this to Jeremiah in terms pointing to great violence: "Those of my people who listen to what the false prophets prophesy will be laid out on the streets of Jerusalem by the famine and by the sword. There will not be one person to bury them, not them, not their wives, not their sons, not their daughters. I will pour out upon them all their wickedness . . ." (14:16).

These particularly violent words are left incomplete; God interrupts his sentence and suddenly confesses what the violence hides, his tears. If there is no one left to bury the people, it remains for God to perform this task alone, but, he suddenly confesses to Jeremiah, this morbid duty will be accomplished in tears . . . The passage tells us what God finally reveals, to this point kept hidden in his modest reserve: the tears of his wounded heart.

Reader friend, many people today are shocked by God's violence in the Old Testament. This we understand, but here we have a passage that wonderfully lifts the veil on the true nature of this violence; it is nothing but the expression of his pain, the cry of his tears . . . The wrath of God is the violence of his tears!

God weeps "night and day," which is to say, as long as his people suffer! The seraphim, who likewise acclaim God "night and day" (Rev 4:8), do so veiling their faces (Isa 6:2); they, no more than we, though so close to God, look at their Lord! Modesty prevents them looking at him in his tears! Never, though, do they cease to cry out, "Holy, holy, holy is the Lord . . ."

Hidden tears

Another passage in Jeremiah also tells us of God's tears: "If you will not listen, my soul will weep in the secret places, it will be nothing but tears because of pride.[2] My eyes will run down with tears because the flock of the Lord has gone into captivity" (Jer 13:17). In Jeremiah, this text comes before the one we have just looked at, but I have kept it until later because it is not at first clear who we should think is speaking. If we attach the verse directly to those immediately preceding it, it is Jeremiah who is speaking and pursing a discourse addressed to the people. On the

2. Translating the French. (Trans.)

other hand, if it belongs to the following verses, then God is speaking, adding to what his prophet has said: "If you will not listen (that is, to what Jeremiah says to you), then my soul will weep . . ."

Generally speaking, Christian commentators and translators think that it is Jeremiah who is speaking, whereas Jewish commentators think it is God.[3] This difference in interpretation is indicative of Christian reticence to envisage God as able to weep. Greek influence marked Christianity much more strongly than it did Judaism, which knew how to understand God's confession.

A close look at the verse inclines me to rank myself with the Jewish commentators.

That God would designate himself in the first person ("*my* soul," "*my* eye"), and then in the third ("the flock of *the Lord*" rather than "*my* flock") does not present a problem; this way of speaking is very frequent in the prophetic literature.

What is striking, by contrast, is the expression "my soul shall weep." Nowhere else in the Old Testament is there any mention of a soul that weeps. No doubt this is a way of saying that the tears in question are deeper than tears from the eyes. When tears appear in the eyes they can be superficial or even counterfeit. However, tears from the soul can have nothing artificial about them; they are true and more profound.

"My soul shall weep": if no one else in the Bible talks like this, no doubt it is because the one who speaks here weeps like no one in the world can!

The Hebrew expression that follows, translated as, "it will be nothing but tears," is another turn of phrase

3. See the Babylonian Talmud, Haguigah 5b.

found nowhere else in the Old Testament. A verb is used here which is not used otherwise; again, the person who is speaking here weeps like no one else can weep!

Would these tears unlike others be God's? I believe so and believe it gladly! The idea that this is purely anthropomorphism may be difficult to avoid, but how else is God's pain to be expressed? The best solution is undoubtedly the one we find here, to use human images but employing expressions never used for people. God weeps, but not like us, in a way that is beyond us . . . It is beyond description, but nonetheless speaks to us with unparalleled strength.

It is even more indescribable in that we must not forget that God rejoices too, and that his joy is so deep that it goes far beyond any human joy. God rejoices as no one in the world could ever rejoice. He rejoices unceasingly, night and day, at each act of love between his creatures, at each humble word or attitude. He is carried away with joy each time a lost sheep is found . . . We need to know how to hold both thoughts together if we are to take account of this double reality, that God both weeps and rejoices without ceasing. We mustn't adopt a way of speaking which is overly anthropomorphic since it does't help an awareness of the twofold reality of the divine. While we will speak here only of God's tears, we understand that his joy is a reality just as deep.

"Pride"; it is this that brings God to tears! Not "your pride," but "pride," which is to say pride in general without reference to nation. As long as there is pride in the earth, God will weep, night and day, without ceasing . . . which, I am sorry to say, means that he will weep until the end of time! Pride is an inner leprosy so profoundly incrusted onto the heart of man! It began in the Garden of Eden when

Adam and Eve proposed to be like God. Since then, day and night, God has not ceased to weep . . .

The threefold mention of tears in this one verse, this linguistic redundancy, tells of the most serious nature of pride in God's eyes: "My soul shall weep . . . it will be wholly tears . . . my eye will run down with tears."

"My soul shall weep in the secret places": the modesty, the reserve of God is wonderfully apparent here. God's weeping is constant, certainly, but it is always hidden. In Jeremiah's presence he speaks of his tears for the first time, but his reserve remains; the tears remain hidden. This reserve is at the same time a protection to us; anyone, indeed, who was to surprise God weeping would not be able to bear it . . .

Above all, it is from the prideful that God hides his tears. Jeremiah, no doubt, was sufficiently humble to hear God's confiding words, but this doesn't mean he ever saw God weep.

Our pride will always leave us blind to the, for us, invisible tears of God, but it is good, as we read Jeremiah, to realize that it is to this God, a God who sheds tears over us, that we are drawing near in each of our steps of repentance. When the prodigal son came home to his father, didn't the father fall on his son's neck to hide his tears from him?

More hidden tears

"O that my head were a fountain and my eyes, springs of tears, that I might cry day and night for the slain of the daughter of my people! O that I lived in some wayfarers' cabin far off in the wilderness!" (Jer 9:1).

This verse comes first in the book of Jeremiah, before the two discussed above, but the tone is the same in each case; however I am not going to go into this verse in detail because it is still more difficult than the others to know who is speaking.

Was it Jeremiah? I don't know, but, if it was, his pain is so close to God's that one can understand why it would have been to this prophet that God chose to speak of his own pain, his own tears, and his desire to hide from those for whom he was weeping.

Was it God? I don't know, but if it was, he is so discreet as to hide his admission in the words of his prophet and his tears in the tears of Jeremiah!

This happy imprecision so respects the modesty of God! The veil is not to be lifted any further!

"The hope of Israel"

This phrase, which designates God, is found nowhere other than in Jeremiah (14:8, 17:13, 50:7). It is an untranslatable expression since it includes a play on words, the effect of which, again, is to veil God's tears. The context certainly invites the translation common to all our versions, "the hope of Israel," but we should know that the word translated by "hope," *miqwe*, also means "a reservoir of water," and was used in particular for the basin for cleansing located at the entrance to the sanctuary. In a veiled way, God is described as a repository of water so vast as to cleanse all the people! The water in the laver never became stagnant; from God there is a never ceasing stream of cleansing water. The allusion to tears is more than discreet, but it is there, just the same.

The secret place

"My soul will weep in the secret places," as we heard God say (Jer 13:17). What are we to do with this information volunteered by God himself? What could this hidden place be?

There is a great temptation to wish to know more, but at the same time this is to somewhat abuse God's modesty. His hiding place is his secret, a mystery to be respected. It is really better for us to leave it there and not wish to know any more; rather, we should be seeking how to avoid causing God still more tears . . .

Nevertheless, we do find in Judaism a boldness that sought to find out the mystery of God's hiding place, not out of some misplaced curiosity that would be unwholesome and unwelcome, but out of genuine love! This is why we can pay attention to their audacity; it seems to me to have been inspired by the only true spirit of love, the Holy Spirit himself; he is the only one who can guide human love into the hidden depths of God, just as the apostle Paul says (1 Cor 2:10).

In order to hide himself, God has no need to go beyond the galaxies to the end of the universe. Not at all, say the rabbis! There is a much more secure hiding place — in the most secret recesses of the human soul . . .

There could be no more secure place for God because it is exactly here that the darkness is thickest; the darkness of the human soul is denser than a black hole because of the pride that envelops it; so intensely in fact that God can hide there without the human gaze being able to discern his presence. There indeed God can weep in secret.

That said, it shows how wonderfully humble God must be that he would hide himself somewhere so dishonorable! Humbly he hides his tears, there in the very residence of pride! How humble he is!

By choosing such a place to hide it becomes apparent that God's way of doing things is one of extreme love, and is altogether overwhelming! In fact, as he hides in the darkness of the soul, God in his humility comes to combat and throw out pride, causing it to melt away like wax in a fire. Pride cannot bear humility any more than wax can survive fire. God in his unfathomable love weeps for our pride and chooses to weep in the very place of pride's stronghold; his goal, wonderfully, to deliver us. The humble tears of God chase away pride and at the same time cleanse us of its foul defilement. God does not judge our soul, benighted though it is in pride, but delivers it, enlightens it, cares, heals, disinfects and cleanses it . . . in the silence of his tears . . . What love!

This is why, despite the impurity of our pride, we are able to shed pure tears; the clean, pure tears that flow in the midst of our unclean tears come from deep in our soul, from God himself as he hides his tears in ours . . . And when finally our heart is entirely cleansed of pride, then comes the fulfillment of the promise announced by Jesus: Blessed are the pure in heart, for they shall see God.

Go into the secret place

In a most beautiful section of the Sermon on the Mount, in which he inveighs against the ostentatious prayers of the proud, Jesus exhorts us to pray humbly, calling us to a process of the greatest importance: go, he tells us, into the most secret place, which is to say, as the Fathers well understood, into the most secret recess of your soul, of your heart. Then, Jesus continues, shut the door without delay; the one you seek is already there, awaiting you; your heavenly Father is there in the secret of your heart, in the deepest place of your soul (Matt 6:6).

For Jesus, clearly, God can be both in heaven and in our heart, entirely present but inaccessible in heaven and entirely present in the inaccessible depths of our hearts. God remains hidden in the secret of our heart, in silence, listening to the prayer of whoever is looking for him.

"Your Father is there," says Jesus; unmentioned though, and not unveiled by Jesus, are the tears God weeps. Jesus never speaks of them. It is not that he was unaware of what had been a revelation to Jeremiah, but that he didn't wish to talk about it, out of respect for his Father's privacy. As we shall see later, he has a different way to reveal these hidden tears. However, before going further into the Gospel, we will pause for a while on the matter of the secret place of our souls where God is concealed.

"If you will not listen," God says, "my soul shall weep in the secret places." The nature of God's chosen hiding-place has a lot to say about repentance. Anyone who through pride does not listen to God knows nothing of all this, but God weeps secretly in their heart. A person may ignore it and perhaps even mock. There is no point saying more since they will never listen and will disdain even a God this humble.

By contrast, a person who becomes aware of his or her pride and begins to seek God for healing of it, has no need to look very far. They need only look within, and in doing so they draw near to God who is already there in the depths of their soul, there, where he weeps in secret. And should this prideful person actually begin to shed tears over their pride, they may be sure that their tears are mingled with the tears of God who already forgives and cleanses. The bitter tears of the proud person begin to become sweet at the moment God indicates his forgiveness, as we learned from John Climacus.

The Septuagint translation

Before we return to Christ, so careful in consideration of his Father's tears, we will turn back to the Old Testament Greek of the Septuagint, which veiled the tears of God for the same reason: respect for God's feelings.

The Septuagint translation was made around the second century before our era by Jews who wished to make the Bible accessible to the Greek world of the period, and to make their God known. The translation was undertaken by men who were perfectly informed about the Greek mentality of the time, so when it came to translating the verses from Jeremiah that mention God's tears, they pulled back, not wishing to offend Greek sensibilities. The Greeks were so closed off to the idea that a god might cry that the translators preferred to paper over something that might provoke rejection or mockery; their objective, to preserve the honor of God. Out of respect for God, their translation introduced a slight modification, replacing one possessive pronoun with another; this was enough to have the tears of God replaced by the people's.

Thus we find in the Septuagint for Jeremiah 14:17, not, "Say to them that *my* eyes run down with tears, night and day . . ." but "Say to them that *your* eyes will run with tears, night and day . . ." The same occurs with 13.17: "If you will not listen, *your* soul will weep in secret; because of pride *your* eyes will shed tears . . ."

When it came to 9:1, there was no need for any change because the "mistake" would be so great that any good Greek reader, formed by the Greek spirit, would be sure that it was Jeremiah who wept.

The Septuagint itself was translated into Copt, Syrian, Aramaean, Ethiopian . . . so the whole eastern Christian world knew nothing about God and tears. The Vulgate translation into Latin was an exception since it was translated from the Hebrew, so the Latin Fathers had at least he possibility of recognizing them, but to my knowledge, nonetheless, no Latin Father speaks of them; this would seem to indicate the degree to which the Greek spirit affected the Latin world too.

Among all the Fathers there is, however, a remarkable exception. There may be others, but I don't know of them since my knowledge of the Fathers is not that extensive. While still hoping to discover another reference, I can, however, pass on what I have found in Macarius the Great; it causes me to marvel to the highest degree.

The tears of God in Macarius

We have today a whole series of homilies ascribed to Macarius the Great, the founder of Scetis in the Egyptian desert in the fourth century. Modern criticism considers these homilies not to be by Macarius but by one of his disciples, but, after all, this does not matter much since it doesn't change what they say. To simplify these remarks, we will speak here of Macarius, knowing that we are perhaps dealing with an anonymous author, one so humble that he did not wish to leave us his name! Happy man!

A reading of these homilies shows clearly that their author was Syrian; we will not go into detail, but the theology of the author is typically Syrian, which is very important for our purposes, since the Syrians were Semites. Their mentality was much closer to the Jews than it was to the Greeks, and this is enough to understand how Macarius could dare to think of God as able to weep, and then dare to say it. Indeed he speaks of it without imagining that there might be anything shocking about this. Quite the contrary, as we will see! He discusses the subject in two homilies, the first and the thirtieth.

Macarius' first homily

"When the body of a sick person is unable to receive nourishment, his friends, his family and his acquaintances despair of his healing and weep for him. In the same way, God and the holy angels weep over souls which refuse the heavenly nourishment of the Spirit, and live in their corruption" (1.11).

The remarkable thing about this passage is that the relationship pictured between God and man is not of a moral, juridical, legal nature . . . Man's "corruption" is not described under the rubric of sin and hence God's judgment, but as a malady, attracting his compassion. All idea of human culpability is set to the side in order to focus on friendship with God, who is concerned for our spiritual well-being and visits us as a familiar. His compassion brings him to tears, and all the holy angels with him. There is even a quasi despair on God's part at being unable to force feed the person who deliberately refuses all spiritual nourishment; humanity is free, and God weeps over our suicidal use of this liberty.

This extract from the homily speaks wonderfully of God's tears of compassion and his friendship towards us. He weeps in silence and the whole of heaven weeps with him.

Macarius' thirtieth homily

"*On the day Adam fell, God came to Paradise to walk and look. He wept, we may say, when he saw Adam, and said, 'What good you have left behind to choose such evil! What glory you have lost to be clothed with such shame!*

What darkness you now have, what ugliness, what stench! What light you have lost, and what darkness covers you!'

When Adam died and fell far from God, the Creator wept over him. The angels, all the Powers, the heavens, the earth and all creatures lamented his death and his fall; they saw the one who had been given them as king become a slave of wicked, enemy powers, and his soul thus enveloped in darkness. He had indeed fallen into the power of the Prince of darkness. This is the very man who was covered in wounds by brigands and left half-dead when he went down from Jerusalem to Jericho.

Lazarus too, who the Lord raised when the stench of his body was too great for anyone to go near the tomb, he too was a symbol of Adam, whose soul stank too, full of blackness and darkness.

But you, when you hear of Adam, of the wounded traveller, of Lazarus, you should not allow your mind to fly away, but should hold the thought, considering your own soul; you also have the same wounds, the same stink of death, the same darkness. We are all, indeed, children of this darkened race, and we all participate in the same stench. The suffering Adam underwent, we endure too; we too, we who belong to his race. The suffering which has become our portion is just what Isaiah describes: 'Nothing but wounds, bruises, putrifying sores which are not healed or soothed with ointments or bandaged' (Isa 1:6). Look at this untreatable wound with which we are smitten; only the Lord can heal it.... Only he, when he comes, heals this untreatable wound in the soul" (30.7-8).

I will make no more than a few remarks on this wonderful text.

The opening of the passage takes us back to the Garden of Eden, to the moment Adam fell by listening to the serpent. God comes to the Garden to stroll, says Macarius, referring to Genesis 3.8. For we western Christians, there is a need to read and re-read this typically eastern text, to disengage our spirit from the interpretation to which our latinate spirits are habituated, which envisages the fall purely from a juridical angle, presenting it as a sin meriting God's sanction.

"Where are you?" cries God in the Garden of Eden as he sought Adam. The God Macarius describes is not a police officer or a judge interrogating the accused; he is a God in tears, questioning a wounded man, just like the man wounded by brigands and left half-dead on the Jerusalem–Jericho road (Luke 10:30).

"He wept, so to speak . . ." Macarius is carefully with what he says, very correctly. This "so to speak" discounts any anthropomorphism and allows us to go further into the text towards the unfathomable, to speak of the indescribable.

In the first homily, God weeps over a friend in ill health and we find more of the same here. There is no question anywhere in this extract from the thirtieth homily of a fault or sin. On the contrary, Adam is presented as a patient with an "incurable wound." Macarius is in the direct line of oriental Christian theology which does not present the fall as an issue of guilt and punishment, but of wounding and healing. We might say that when he bit into the fruit, Adam was bitten by the serpent with a mortal wound, the "incurable wound" the Lord comes to heal. Macarius sees God as both a physician and a tearful friend. Rather than the aspect of pardon and cleansing, Macarius proposes healing and disinfection. The God of Macarius perfectly resembles the God of Jeremiah.

Not once in this text does Macarius mention pride, but the rest of his homilies reveal the incurable wound of the soul that had struck Adam as indeed pride; we thus get back to what we learned from Jeremiah (13:17).

Macarius does not stress the point, but we realize that God, in fact, was the first in the world to have wept. Before Adam's fall there was nothing that could have caused tears. Adam's fall is the first event that could cause tears to fall, and it is for God himself to shed them. In this way, God is the source of tears. Before humanity shed its first tear, God's began to flow.

Adam, Macarius specifies, is each of us. We are of his race, his descendants, subject like him to the same evil, bruised by the same wound, so much so that God weeps over each of us. Each of our crises of pride causes God to weep; therefore from that time he has not ceased to shed tears, "night and day," as Jeremiah says. As long as the proud inhabit the earth, God will weep. This truly is as much as to say that he will weep until the final day!

The first person to have wept, God is gravely at risk of also being the last!

God weeps over Adam, indeed in his presence, even while Adam is unable to see the tears, simply because he is thrust into thick darkness. Macarius insists on this "bitter, malign" darkness; it is what makes God invisible. God has no need to hide; he is already hidden from Adam's eyes by the darkness.

The tears of Christ

As we read Macarius, we ask ourselves how this Church Father came to ponder the tears of God, when the Syrian Bible, translated from the Greek, never mentions them. Indeed, how did he come to speak as he did, which is to say, so confidently, as of fact, rather than hypothesis or bold suggestion? Macarius doesn't explain himself on this point, but his text makes it clear what impelled him to speak like this.

Before saying that we are similar to Adam, Macarius compares Lazarus and Adam, even seeing Lazarus as a "symbol of Adam." The parallel between the two figures is portrayed in such a way that the wounding to Adam exhales the stench of a cadaver, and the darkness into which he is plunged is just as dense as the darkness Lazarus knew in his tomb. Macarius had in mind the text of Genesis, and illuminates it from the chapter of John recounting the raising of Lazarus; in the gospel passage, we are told that "Jesus wept" (John 11:35). The tears of Christ; here we are left in no doubt as to what prompted Macarius' reflection and meditation.

Staying close to Macarius' thought, we might say that Jesus was weeping for his friend now engulfed in thick darkness, his friend who had been wounded with an incurable wound that bound him to death. For Macarius, Jesus' tears over his friend Lazarus reveal God's tears over his friend, Adam. I can't see any other explanation than this and find it altogether inspired, perfectly in line with Genesis, the Gospels and everythingl God said to Jeremiah.

In John 11:35, the verb which describes Jesus' tears is a verb not found elsewhere in the New Testament (*dakruein*). Jesus, according to St. John, weeps in a way no one else could. No one else? Only God, in the end, who himself weeps as no one else can.

Revelatory tears

In the Biblical world it was acceptable for a woman to cry in public, and it was even required of her in the ritual of funeral lamentation. A man, however, had to hide if he wished to weep; Joseph hid (Gen 42:24, 43:30), David hid (2 Sam 12.16) — a man does not show his tears. Strangely though, with Lazarus' death, Jesus wept without dissembling his tears. All those around witnessed this, and the evangelist even says that the Jews saw in these tears the extent of Jesus' love for Lazarus: "See how he loved him!" (John 11:36).

Did Jesus lack a proper sense of shame? I think not. The tears he shed were in no way similar to Martha's and Mary's (11:33). John chose to describe Jesus' tears with a unique verb, as if to invite a search elsewhere for a point of reference. Jesus was not weeping to demonstrate his love for Lazarus, but to reveal other tears, tears until then shed in secret and conscientiously hidden. Jesus never spoke of God's tears out of consideration for his Father; he was however easy about weeping himself, without hiding and without commenting on his own tears, except, perhaps, for what he would say some days later, most discreetly, "Whoever sees me, sees him who sent me" (12:45), and later again, "He who has seen me has seen the Father" (14:9).

He who has seen my tears has seen my Father's . . .

As he contemplated the tears of Christ shed over his friend Lazarus, Macarius saw past them to the tears shed by God over us all, his friends! The soul darkened by the darkness of the heart can now contemplate the invisible and marvel: God loves us to such a degree that he weeps over us: "See how he loved him!" He loves us enough to snatch us from the grip of death, thus healing the incurable wound . . .

Jesus weeps over Jerusalem

Luke, in his Gospel, describes another episode in which Jesus began to weep (19:41). This passage offers us wonderful points of comparison with what we found in Jeremiah.

Through the texts in Jeremiah, we found God weeping over the city of Jerusalem strewn with corpses left without burial. Many centuries later, Jesus announced a new fall for Jerusalem in terms just as severe as those used by God in Jeremiah: "The days are coming when your enemies will surround you with trenches; they will shut you in and cut you off; they will destroy you, you and your children in the midst of you; they will not leave one stone on another, because you did not know the time when you were visited" (Luke 19:43-44). Jesus' severity contains a hidden anger, similar to God's. Like God, Jesus began to weep over the city doomed to destruction . . .

No more than Jerusalem had actually seen God weep in Jeremiah's time did she see Jesus weep over her; only the disciples were witnesses of their master's tears. Jesus didn't hide from their sight so they were able to contemplate through his tears the tears of his Father . . .

Jesus never ventured to speak of his Father's tears, but in silence he demonstrated them . . .

It was in tears that Jesus announced the worst catastrophes that were to befall Jerusalem (19: 43–44), and it was with the same tears that he so shortly after chased the merchants out of the Temple (19:45)!

When we uncover and realize this about Christ's anger, we can no longer speak as we did about the anger of God.

Another text from Macarius

There is another text which we have not touched on yet, another text from Macarius as paraphrased in the tenth century by one Symeon Metaphraste, a text in which we don't really know how much is Macarius and how much Symeon. Here is the passage:

> *"When we hear the word of the Kingdom and we are led to tears, we should not hold back the tears we are shedding; we should not stop up our ears, since they have heard correctly; nor our eyes, which have seen things as they are; and neither should we think that we have gone far enough yet. There are other ears, other eyes and other tears, as there is another way of seeing and another soul, which is the divine Spirit, the heavenly Spirit himself, who listens and who weeps, who prays, who knows, and who does the will of God in truth.*
>
> *The Lord, when he promised the apostles the overwhelming gift of the Spirit, said, indeed: 'I am going away, but the Comforter, the Holy Spirit whom the Father will send in my name, he will teach you all things'. It is therefore he, the Holy Spirit, who will pray, and he who will weep.*
>
> *When, in accordance with the promise, the Comforter came on the day of Pentecost, and the power of the good Spirit took up residence in the soul of the apostles, they were totally delivered from the covering of malice, the passions disappeared and the eyes of their hearts were opened."*

This text has the great positive of seeing God's location as in the human soul, as we saw in the Jewish tradition too. It is there that God weeps, or, more precisely, there that the Holy Spirit weeps. We can't say whether it is Macarius or Symeon who makes the distinction, and it doesn't matter; whatever the case, we should not stop at these tears that we shed, in the sense that our attention should not be fixed on ourselves. What matters is to look beyond our tears to others of infinitely more importance, the tears of the Holy Spirit, who comes to weep in us, thus mingling his tears with ours.

The Holy Spirit weeps and the Son too, together with the Father; the three persons of the Holy Trinity are joined in indescribable tears . . .

The silence of the Book of Revelation

You will remember both my amazement and my question — how is it that our unclean heart is able to shed pure, clean tears? Reader friend, what I believe is that this whole thing comes from God who weeps in secret in the depths of our heart, transforming our unclean tears, making them pure. If our own pure tears purify and cleanse us, as John Climacus says, it is not because they have this virtue of themselves but because this property is given them by the tears of God which are mingled with them, the tears of the thrice Holy Trinity . . .

This is the way the tears of Most Holy Love cleanse us; they heal, disinfect and cleanse the incurable wound to our soul . . .

In the book of Revelation, we are told that at the opening of the seventh seal, "there was silence in heaven for about half an hour (8:1). In this book so full of movement and sound and words of every type, a silence as long as this attracts our whole attention. What is going on that heaven should observe such a deep silence?

It seems to me that the reason lies in the event announced just before, in the immediately preceding verse. God wipes away every tear from the eyes of those who have passed through the great tribulation . . . The Lord has come down from his throne and passes before each of his own, to wipe away each tear in silence . . .

It is the silence of heaven contemplating this gesture of tenderness of the Humble and Most Holy Love . . .

Blessed are the pure in heart, for they see God . . .

As we see him thus consoling all the afflicted, new tears begin to flow, the sweet tears of eternal well-being . . .